A Retreat With
Job and Julian of Norwich

Trusting That All Will Be Well

Carol Luebering

St. Anthony Messenger Press

Cincinnati, Ohio

Other titles in the
A Retreat With... *Series:*

Excerpts from *The Bereaved Parent* by Harriet Sarnoff Schiff.
Copyright ©1977 by Harriet Sarnoff Schiff. Reprinted by
permission of Crown Publishers, Inc. Copyright ©1948, 1976 by
Crown Publishers, Inc. Reprinted by permission of Crown
Publishers, Inc.

Excerpts from *A Treasury of Jewish Folklore* by Nathan Ausubel.
Copyright ©1947 and renewed 1974 by Crown Publishers, Inc.
Reprinted by permission of Crown Publishers, Inc.

Cover illustrations by Steve Erspamer, S.M.
Cover and book design by Mary Alfieri

ISBN 0-86716-227-9

Copyright ©1995, Carol Luebering

Published by St. Anthony Messenger Press
Printed in the U.S.A.

Contents

Introducing A Retreat With...

Twenty years ago I made a weekend retreat at a Franciscan house on the coast of New Hampshire. The retreat director's opening talk was as lively as a long-range weather forecast. He told us how completely God loves each one of us—without benefit of lively anecdotes or fresh insights.

As the friar rambled on, my inner critic kept up a sotto voce commentary: "I've heard all this before." "Wish he'd say something new that I could chew on." "That poor man really doesn't have much to say." Ever hungry for manna yet untasted, I devalued any experience of hearing the same old thing.

After a good night's sleep, I awoke feeling as peaceful as a traveler who has at last arrived safely home. I walked across the room toward the closet. On the way I passed the sink with its small framed mirror on the wall above. Something caught my eye like an unexpected presence. I turned, saw the reflection in the mirror and said aloud, "No wonder he loves me!"

This involuntary affirmation stunned me. What or whom had I seen in the mirror? When I looked again, it was "just me," an ordinary person with a lower-than-average reservoir of self-esteem. But I knew that in the initial vision I had seen God-in-me breaking through like a sudden sunrise.

At that moment I knew what it meant to be made in

the divine image. I understood right down to my size eleven feet what it meant to be loved exactly as I was. Only later did I connect this revelation with one granted to the Trappist monk-writer Thomas Merton. As he reports in *Conjectures of a Guilty Bystander*, while standing all unsuspecting on a street corner one day, he was overwhelmed by the "joy of being...a member of a race in which God Himself became incarnate.... There is no way of telling people that they are all walking around shining like the sun."

As an absentminded homemaker may leave a wedding ring on the kitchen windowsill, so I have often mislaid this precious conviction. But I have never forgotten that particular retreat. It persuaded me that the Spirit rushes in where it will. Not even a boring director or a judgmental retreatant can withstand the "violent wind" that "fills the entire house" where we dwell in expectation (see Acts 2:2).

So why deny ourselves any opportunity to come aside awhile and rest on holy ground? Why not withdraw from the daily web that keeps us muddled and wound? Wordsworth's complaint is ours as well: "The world is too much with us." There is no flu shot to protect us from infection by the skepticism of the media, the greed of commerce, the alienating influence of technology. We need retreats as the deer needs the running stream.

An Invitation

This book and its companions in the *A Retreat With...* series from St. Anthony Messenger Press are designed to meet that need. They are an invitation to choose as director some of the most powerful, appealing and wise mentors our faith tradition has to offer.

Our directors come from many countries, historical eras and schools of spirituality. At times they are teamed to sing in close harmony (for example, Francis de Sales, Jane de Chantal and Aelred of Rievaulx on spiritual friendship). Others are paired to kindle an illuminating fire from the friction of their differing views (such as Augustine of Hippo and Mary Magdalene on human sexuality). All have been chosen because, in their humanness and their holiness, they can help us grow in self-knowledge, discernment of God's will and maturity in the Spirit.

Inviting us into relationship with these saints and holy ones are inspired authors from today's world, women and men whose creative gifts open our windows to the Spirit's flow. As a motto for the authors of our series, we have borrowed the advice of Dom Frederick Dunne to the young Thomas Merton. Upon joining the Trappist monks, Merton wanted to sacrifice his writing activities lest they interfere with his contemplative vocation. Dom Frederick wisely advised, "Keep on writing books that make people love the spiritual life."

That is our motto. Our purpose is to foster (or strengthen) friendships between readers and retreat directors—friendships that feed the soul with wisdom, past and present. Like the scribe "trained for the kingdom of heaven," each author brings forth from his or her storeroom "what is new and what is old" (Matthew 13:52).

The Format

The pattern for each *A Retreat With...* remains the same; readers of one will be in familiar territory when they move on to the next. Each book is organized as a seven-session retreat that readers may adapt to their own schedules or to the needs of a group.

Day One begins with an anecdotal introduction called "Getting to Know Our Directors." Readers are given a telling glimpse of the guides with whom they will be sharing the retreat experience. A second section, "Placing Our Directors in Context," will enable retreatants to see the guides in their own historical, geographical, cultural and spiritual settings.

Having made the human link between seeker and guide, the authors go on to "Introducing Our Retreat Theme." This section clarifies how the guide(s) are especially suited to explore the theme and how the retreatant's spirituality can be nourished by it.

After an original "Opening Prayer" to breathe life into the day's reflection, the author, speaking with and through the mentor(s), will begin to spin out the theme. While focusing on the guide's own words and experience, the author may also draw on Scripture, tradition, literature, art, music, psychology or contemporary events to illuminate the path.

Each day's session is followed by reflection questions designed to challenge, affirm and guide the reader in integrating the theme into daily life. A "Closing Prayer" brings the session full circle and provides a spark of inspiration for the reader to harbor until the next session.

Days Two through Six begin with "Coming Together in the Spirit" and follow a format similar to Day One. Day Seven weaves the entire retreat together, encourages a continuation of the mentoring relationship and concludes with "Deepening Your Acquaintance," an envoi to live the theme by God's grace, the director(s)' guidance and the retreatant's discernment. A closing section of Resources serves as a larder from which readers may draw enriching books, videos, cassettes and films.

We hope readers will experience at least one of those memorable "No wonder God loves me!" moments. And we hope that they will have "talked back" to the mentors, as good friends are wont to do.

A case in point: There was once a famous preacher who always drew a capacity crowd to the cathedral. Whenever he spoke, an eccentric old woman sat in the front pew directly beneath the pulpit. She took every opportunity to mumble complaints and contradictions— just loud enough for the preacher to catch the drift that he was not as wonderful as he was reputed to be. Others seated down front glowered at the woman and tried to shush her. But she went right on needling the preacher to her heart's content.

When the old woman died, the congregation was astounded at the depth and sincerity of the preacher's grief. Asked why he was so bereft, he responded, "Now who will help me to grow?"

All of our mentors in *A Retreat With...* are worthy guides. Yet none would seek retreatants who simply said, "Where you lead, I will follow. You're the expert." In truth, our directors provide only half the retreat's content. Readers themselves will generate the other half.

As general editor for the retreat series, I pray that readers will, by their questions, comments, doubts and decision-making, fertilize the seeds our mentors have planted.

And may the Spirit of God rush in to give the growth.

Gloria Hutchinson
Series Editor
Conversion of Saint Paul, 1995

Getting to Know Our Directors

Introducing Julian

The black curtain emblazoned with a white cross stirs in the spring breeze. The yellow cat sitting on the windowsill leaps away at the approach of the stranger who whispers his pain to the unseen figure behind the curtain. A warm, womanly voice addresses him: "All will be well. You will see yourself that every kind of thing will be well."

Behind the curtained window is a small cell, a tiny cubicle built against the wall of the church in Norwich, England, dedicated to St. Julian. We know its occupant only by the name of the church: Julian of Norwich, we call her. She is an anchoress, a laywoman bound by solemn vows to remain "anchored"—to abide in her cell for the rest of her life. The *Ancrene Riwle* (Anchorine Rule) governs her days. It prescribes a daily regime of fasting and prayer. She explores Scripture and prays the psalms. She plies her needle, making and mending clothes for the poor. The rule also permits her the services of a maidservant and, to keep the rodent population down, the company of a cat. (In a chapel window in Norwich Cathedral a cat sits at Julian's feet, staring with feline disdain at passersby.)

For support she depends on whatever resources she previously owned, the generosity of the townspeople and bequests. (People are still mentioning her in their wills as late as 1416, when Julian is in her eighth decade.)

Julian's story begins for us where she herself chose to begin it: on May 8 or 13, 1373. (Numerals *VIII* and *XIII* are easily confused in hand-copied medieval manuscripts.) In her thirty-first year at the time, Julian had what some today might call a near-death experience. Struck down by a fever, she felt death approach; the lower half of her body was already bereft of feeling and her sight was darkening. Her family sent for a priest to give her the last rites. He held a crucifix before her eyes with the invitation, *"I have brought the image of your saviour; look at it and take comfort from it."*[1] As she felt life ebb from the upper part of her body and gasped for every breath, the only light she could see rested on the crucifix.

Suddenly her pain vanished, and she saw blood trickling from beneath the crown of thorns on the figure of the crucified Christ. In a vision Julian watched Jesus suffer and die. The visions continued—sixteen in all—into the next day, revealing to her the unfathomable depths of God's love.

To everyone's amazement, Julian recovered from the illness that had nearly carried her off. She did not recover from her visions. The very core of her being had been seared by her experience of divine love. No cozy fire this, contained in a hearth by which she could warm herself, but a flame such as the prophet Jeremiah describes:

> ...something like a burning fire
>   shut up in my bones;
> I am weary with holding it in,
>   and I cannot.[2]

She wrote down her "showings," as she called them— first a short draft and then, after twenty years of reflection on her experience, a longer, more theological version. Her *Revelations of Divine Love* is the oldest surviving manuscript written by a woman in English, the language of her contemporary, Chaucer.

Sensing a call to spread the flame into hearts waiting like dry tinder for a spark, Julian pledged herself to the solitary life of an anchoress. Why did a woman with such a sense of mission not seek out a convent, where she could at least share her experience with a company of sisters? Her chosen life included vowed celibacy and obedience, especially to the bishop, just as a nun's did. Perhaps the answer lies in the years she does not tell us about, the first thirty of her life. She could have been a widow in an era when women's monasteries often accepted only virgins. (That was apparently true of the lone community in Norwich.) She may have lost a husband—even children—in the repeated visitations of the Black Death or to any of the other diseases and disasters that set life expectancy so low in the fourteenth century. It may be that the straining toward God she attests to in the opening lines of her *Revelations* was conceived by grief.

Whatever the reason, she took her vows as an anchoress in the presence of her bishop. In a dramatic ceremony, she lay motionless while a Requiem Mass was sung, a funeral liturgy for a woman now dead to her previous existence. Then the bishop led her to her cell and ritually sealed the door. (A door or window into an adjacent room allowed access to the maidservant who tended Julian's physical needs. The curtained window on the outside of her cell allowed the townspeople to approach her.)

In her anchorage, true solitude often eluded Julian. Her curtained window faced the churchyard and its path; it overlooked the busy river below. Past it paraded the lusty life of a medieval city. Norwich was a bustling port city on the English Channel, second only to London in size. Its wealth derived primarily from the wool trade. (Down in London, a hundred miles south and east, members of an infant Parliament sat on wool sacks as a reminder of that commodity's importance to the country's economy.) Julian's prayers were punctuated by the cries of street peddlers, the lowing and bleating of animals heading to market, the bawdy revelry of holiday processions.

The beloved anchoress and others like her provided small islands of stability, faith and prayer in such a community. People came to these islets of holiness seeking intercession and counsel. The quiet of Julian's cell was often broken by the sobs of the brokenhearted who came to her window for comfort. Comfort them she did, with such maternal tenderness that they called her Mother Julian.

At the other end of the tiny space that was her home for over forty years, a window opened into the church. There Julian became part of the congregation gathered for Eucharist, offering praise and thanksgiving through her beloved Jesus to the God she knew as Father and Mother.

For twenty of those years, Julian reflected on her visions, praying always for deeper insight into what had been revealed to her. In 1393 she completed an expanded version of her *Revelations*. *"I was answered in spiritual understanding,"* she concludes. *" 'What, do you wish to know your Lord's meaning in this thing? Know it well, love was his meaning.' ...So I was taught that love is our Lord's meaning."*[3]

Introducing Job

Julian's companion director of our retreat is a man as familiar with sorrow as anyone who approached her for counsel and comfort. His name is Job.

He sits in the trash dump outside his village. The place is Uz, part of the ancient Canaanite land of Edom, which lies southeast of the land that will be known as holy. Job himself is refuse in the eyes of his community. The hand of God has struck him down.

In a single day messenger after messenger had arrived at his home with the news that his sheep and oxen and camels had been destroyed and his sons and daughters killed. Each concluded with a chilling word: *"I alone have escaped to tell you."*[4] Shortly afterward, his flesh had erupted in loathsome sores.

Only recently Job had enjoyed not only great wealth and a happy family but also the respect of his neighbors. His reputation was that of an upright and God-fearing man. Indeed, his initial response when the first waves of grief swept over him was a prayer of faith: *"[T]he LORD gave, and the LORD has taken away; blessed be the name of the LORD."*[5]

Now he sits in the ashes, scraping his scaling skin with a shard from a broken pot, a pariah avoided by the townspeople. Even the wife who wept with him over their losses has abandoned him. Her parting words, *"Curse God, and die,"*[6] echo bitterly in his ears.

Three figures approach the dump, and Job squints into the sun to make out their faces. Ah, friends from distant parts, friends made in the days when Job led caravans of camels in prosperous commerce. He hails them, and astonishment abruptly halts their stride. Surely this wretched figure cannot be Job! They have heard that great troubles have come upon him and have come to bring whatever comfort is theirs to give. But no rumor has prepared them for the sight of such degradation.

One by one they sink to the ground beside him,

wailing and weeping. And there they remain for seven days and seven nights, unable to find words with which to frame their sympathy. In the end, it is Job who breaks the silence—and he shocks them by cursing the day he was born.

Adherents of faiths that developed after Job's time—Judaism and Christianity—hold Job as a model of submission to God's will. Ezekiel 14:12-20 numbers Job among the outstandingly righteous. James 4:7-11 urges the Christian community to be patient and imitate Job's endurance. Indeed, Job's very name has come to embody the virtue of patience.

But the conversations between Job and his friends reveal very little in the way of patience. They show instead a man of great *impatience* with his friends and with his God, a man whose black despair leads him to wish he had never been born, a man who dares to raise his fist to the sky and challenge his God to face him in a court of law.

Job's words reveal something else, as well: a stubborn faith that God has been his intimate friend. He will not permit his friends to reduce God to an automaton who *must* dispense blessings and punishments in exact accord with human behavior. He will not permit his God to break off their long friendship without explanation. He will wrestle with his pain and with his concept of God until he achieves understanding and peace.

Job's legacy is not patience but endurance. Like Julian, Job persists in his search for God's meaning. And, finally, God breaks the divine silence. Out of a storm God hurls questions like thunderbolts. Does Job know how to create a universe? Does he understand its workings? Can he sustain it? Can Job provide for the living creatures of the earth? Can Job tame chaos and administer divine justice?

Job has to admit the truth: Not even God can explain

God to the human mind. But the God against whom Job has been complaining, the God whose hand has lain heavy upon him, is once again the intimate in whom Job has held constant faith. Job speaks to God, and God speaks to him.

Job has achieved an insight he can own but cannot fully articulate. *"I had heard of you by the ear,/ but now my eye sees you."*[7]

Placing Our Directors in Context

What can a medieval recluse and a man of an ancient village say to twentieth-century people? Although their times were far distant from ours, they were shaped by events and religious attitudes deeply familiar to us. A closer look at their roots will reveal how much we have in common.

Julian's World

Julian's era, the fourteenth century, was in many ways so like our own that historian Barbara Tuchman calls it a "distant mirror." It was a time of endless and terrible warfare, deadly epidemics, social and economic upheaval, and crisis in the Church.

In 1337, five years before Julian's birth, England's King Edward III invaded France to press his claim to his grandfather's throne. Edward's attack marked the beginning of the protracted conflict between England and France now remembered as the Hundred Years' War. It did not end until 1453, a generation or so after Julian was laid to rest.

New and deadly weapons appeared soon after the

conflict began: the deadly accurate English longbow and the cannon. Like any protracted arms buildup, the war drained the royal coffers. Taxes to fund the effort fell heaviest on the poor, but also reduced great fortunes and threatened Church properties as well.

Crowded conditions and poor sanitation had long made cities ripe breeding grounds for disease. In 1349, when Julian was still a little girl, a new horror crossed the British channel from Normandy: the bubonic plague, the Black Death. The stricken died faster than the untouched could bury them; corpses were hastily dumped into mass graves. The plague revisited England seven times over the next century or so and reduced the island's population by at least a third.

Hardest hit were the poor. The thatched roofs of their hovels provided a nesting place for the rats whose fleas carried the deadly germ to those who slept below. Many priests were rightly accused of neglecting their ministry to the sick and dying. Even so, nearly half of England's clergy died in fidelity to their ministry.

Peasants, after burying the children whose labor they needed in the fields, often deserted the lords' lands to which they were bound by feudal law and fled to the cities to seek employment. Landowners, obliged to hire free labor and pressed by rising taxes and prices, appealed to the Royal Council to stabilize wages. The Council responded by reasserting the bondage of serfdom and by fixing wages for free labor at pre-plague levels. Thus was spawned an era of lower-class discontent and outright rebellion.

The fourteenth-century Church was in a state of sad disarray, at the lowest point of its long history. In 1309 Pope Clement V took his papal court where his allegiance lay: to Avignon, France. There wealth and ease quickly bred scandalous corruption.

The competition between French and Italian cardinals led to dual elections. Until 1417 rival claimants to Peter's throne denounced each other. The Council of Pisa, convoked in 1409 to settle the controversy, further muddied the waters by deposing both popes and naming a third.

Not only the papacy lost credibility. Claiming immunity from any but papal taxes and amassing more and more lands by gift and bequest, monasteries of men and women had fallen to mammon. The vows of poverty, chastity and obedience had become largely a joke, even in the orders founded by such earlier reformers as Francis of Assisi and Dominic.

The seeds of the Reformation were being planted. In England John Wycliffe began translating the Bible into his native tongue. He preached the tenets of Protestantism more than a century before Luther.

The hunger for God so ill-served by a corrupt Church also gave rise to mysticism—the direct and intimate experience of God. Among those who claimed such experience was Julian of Norwich, who will share with us in the course of this retreat what was revealed to her.

Job's World

Job's historical roots are more elusive than Julian's. Scripture scholars are unable to date the biblical book that bears his name. Their best-educated guess is that it was written sometime after the Jews returned from exile in Babylon.

In 587 B.C., Nebuchadnezzar's Babylonian armies conquered Judah, the southern half of the kingdom David had united in Israel's glory days. (The Assyrians had wiped out the northern half in 721 B.C.) The invaders razed Jerusalem and marched several thousand of the sad survivors off to slavery in Babylon. Three generations later, Babylon fell to a new power: Persia. Its king, Cyrus, issued an edict permitting the refugees' return to Judah, and in 538 B.C. they streamed homeward.

What awaited them there was hardscrabble poverty and a Jerusalem in ruins. Nothing remained of Solomon's magnificent temple. The returning refugees scratched a meager living from the ravaged land and raised an unimpressive new temple. Their dreams of an Israel restored to the greatness it knew under David and Solomon slowly withered away. And the quest for a new understanding of their relationship with God, begun in the misery of exile, continued.

Against this background of crisis in faith, an unknown poet struggled with the question of human suffering and conceived the biblical Book of Job. Job's arguments with his friends and his God therein challenge Israel's (and many modern believers') dearly-held belief that prosperity and progeny are clear signs of God's approval, that want and woe surely indicate a failure to please God.

Job himself was not the poet's own creation. His story predates Moses, the Exodus and the Covenant—the beginnings of Israel's faith. A righteous sufferer tested by divine powers appears in other ancient Mesopotamian texts. The prophet Ezekiel, writing when Jerusalem's fall was imminent, speaks of three figures from ancient lore who were so righteous they were able to save others: Noah, who saved the whole human race from extinction in the great flood; Daniel (or Danal), an Ugaritic hero known for the efficacy of his prayers; and Job, whose prayer of forgiveness spared his friends God's anger.

Job's story as Ezekiel knew it is the prose that brackets the magnificent poetry of the biblical writer's masterpiece (Job 1:1—2:13; 42:7-17). An adversary, the "satan," dares a powerful god to test the fidelity of a virtuous believer by afflicting him first with the loss of family and fortune, then with bodily affliction. (The satan is not the devil of later belief, but in Mesopotamian thought a lesser god. Israel's faith in the one God transformed the satan into one of God's messengers.)

Job passes the test and the deity rewards him with blessings that surpass what he lost—vaster flocks and greater wealth, another seven sons and three remarkably lovely daughters—and Job lives a long and happy life. The resolution of Job's story confirmed that God does indeed reward virtue with earthly blessings—until an inspired writer began to spin his poetry and gave us the Job who will be our guide in this retreat.

Notes

[1] *Julian of Norwich: Showings*, translated by Edmund Colledge, O.S.A., and James Walsh, S.J. (New York: Paulist Press, 1978), p. 180.

[2] Jeremiah 20:9b.

[3] *Showings*, p. 342.

[4] See Job 1:13-19.

[5] Job 1:21c.

[6] Job 2:9c.

[7] Job 42:5.

Day One
Naming the Pain

Introducing Our Retreat Theme

Job's initial response to his tragedy—"[T]he LORD gave, and the LORD has taken away; blessed be the name of the LORD"[1]—is the ideal toward which faith-filled hearts strain in every age. It is the first response of those who believe in God's goodness. "There is a reason," say the parents of the dead infant, the laid-off worker, the person stricken by a terrible disease. "There is a reason," say those who come to offer comfort. "There must be a reason."

Thus begins the quest for understanding and acceptance, the long journey from pain that is raw and new toward acceptance and peace. That journey is as unique as the searcher who makes it. To be sure, crying out in pain is common to the human condition; each of us was born gasping and wailing in protest. Yet each one's sorrow has a wholly personal dimension that sets it apart from everyone else's.

This retreat offers two companions for that journey: the suffering Job and the mothering Julian. Both of them bear scars. Job was stripped of wealth, family and health; Julian faced the ultimate loss as she felt life itself slipping away from her. Both sought a deeper understanding of God's ways: Job screamed his questions from the trash dump, and Julian pondered her experience in the solitude of her cell.

One sought comfort and one gave it. And both Julian and Job attained deeper understanding of God's ways with the human race. Let them guide your search.

Opening Prayer

> Job, impatient but persistent questioner,
> be with me in my pain.
> Lend me your courage, your determination
> to press my questions on God.
> Support me with your faith
> that God must listen,
> that God will hear the cries of a friend.

> Julian, tender mother,
> wrap me in your warm embrace. Hold me tight
> and comfort my troubled soul.
> Help me believe that,
> in spite of the storms that toss my soul,
> all will indeed be well;
> every manner of thing will be well.

> Wise mentors,
> guide me in my search for healing and peace,
> in my search for the God
> whom this darkness hides from me.

RETREAT SESSION ONE

Your chair is comfortable; settle into it and watch the doorway. The woman standing there turns a warm smile toward you as she enters the room. Mother Julian wears a simple woolen gown; a black veil covers her head. She walks with a firm, sure step, carrying a well-worn Bible. An aura of peace seems to envelop her.

Behind her comes a man in rags. His shoulders are bent as though under a great weight. His face is scarred and immensely sad. He turns toward you and begins to speak. Julian bends forward, listening with her whole body.

Job: Call me not a piece of fiction. Even though I sprang from the mind of a human author rather than from the mind of God, from the flesh of father and mother, I am real. I am the voice of everyone who has ever known pain.

I speak for the bereaved and the bereft. I speak for the abused child cowering in the darkness, for the six million of Israel's faith who died in the Holocaust, for the shoppers shelled in a Sarajevo marketplace, for the thousands massacred in Rwanda.

My tears are as hot on my cheek as those of the families of the disappeared of Central America, the afflicted one moaning against the pain of bone cancer, the battered wife, the child watching her father pour another beer. I bear the weight of depression, that black pall that shrouds the soul. With the dismissed employees of a downsizing company, I mourn the loss of livelihood and pride in work.

I watch the widow weeping at her husband's graveside, the hungry child scavenging in the garbage, the soldiers laughing as they wait their turn with a woman whom they will leave shamed and broken, the late-night jogger fearing the movement of the shadows, the unborn child torn from its mother's womb.

In the days of my prosperity I showed compassion to such as these:

> If I have withheld anything that the poor desired,
>   or have caused the eyes of the widow to fail,
> or have eaten my morsel alone,
>   and the orphan has not eaten from it—
> for from my youth I reared the orphan like a father,
>   and from my mother's womb I guided the
>   widow—
> If I have seen anyone perish for lack of clothing,
>   or a poor person without covering,
> ...then let my shoulder blade fall from my shoulder
>   and let my arm be broken from its socket.[2]

And then I fell into their company. I sat in the trash dump, scraping my skin with a potsherd and wailing all the day.

Julian: Poor Job! We hear the tears of your heart in your voice. I have heard such pain in human voices many, many times before. The good people of Norwich brought their sorrows to the window of my cell. They did not come to me because I am wise—God wot, I am not!—but because they knew that I would listen and sorrow with them.

Job: How fortunate they were! I was shunned by my own townsfolk. They averted their gaze from me, afraid of coming too close to a man cursed by God. Even my wife, who grieved with me when our children died and our fortunes fell, turned away from me when physical affliction struck me down.

A faithful few came and sat with me for a week. What comfort I took from their silent presence! But when we began to converse, their words were like barbs tearing at my already tortured skin, tearing at my heart. They accused me—falsely—of terrible things. They maligned the God with whom I have walked humbly all my years; they turned God into an unfeeling monster incapable of befriending a human being, a cold dispenser of reward and retribution.

Julian: It's true—how often I have seen such a picture. People fear the company of the stricken and the sorrowful. I think they cling too tightly to their own security, their own illusions of safety. For if the hand of God can fall so heavily on a man of proven virtue such as Job, what protection can they claim? To know the extent of one's own vulnerability is to know more than frail hearts can bear. And people feel helpless in the face of suffering they cannot ease. It was for their own protection that they avoided you, Job.

Why the sigh?

Job: Because I knew all that. But knowing didn't help me. How I longed for someone who would hear me!

Julian: We will hear you, Job. Tell us your story.

Job: I was a man blessed by God, a man of means. Five hundred yoke of oxen plowed my fields; five hundred donkeys bore the produce to my barns. My seven thousand sheep grazed on the green hillsides, and three thousand camels carried my goods to the distant corners of Uz and even beyond.

I was a man blessed by God, a man whose walls shook with love and laughter. I had the wife of whom all men dream, a woman of beauty without and within. Her skill with spindle and distaff put other wives to shame. The aroma of the bread baking in her ovens brought wandering strangers to our door, and her hospitality never failed them. A shrewd trader in the marketplace, she managed our household as I managed our fields and flocks, wasting nothing and making everything yield its utmost.

I was a man blessed by God, the father of seven sons and three daughters. Like young olive plants they grew straight and strong, bound together by deep ties of affection. When my sons set up their own households, they would hold feasts in one another's houses, and invite their sisters to join the festivities.

I was a man blessed by God, a man who feared and loved God. I rose early in the morning to sacrifice burnt offerings, lest any unsuspected sin lay hidden in my children's hearts.

I was a man blessed by God until the day when God's hand fell heavy on me. On that day, a horde of Sabeans fell on my oxen and donkeys and servants, and killed them all save the one who brought me the news. That same day lightning struck my sheep and the servants who tended them, killing all save the one who brought me the news. That same day three columns of Chaldeans attacked my caravans, carried off my camels and killed the servants who drove them, all save the one who brought me the news. A tornado struck the house of my eldest son, where all my sons and daughters were feasting, killing everyone save the servant who brought me the news.

What a terrible day that was! With garments rent and

my head shaved, I fell on my knees before God, saying, "*Naked I came from my mother's womb, and naked I shall return there; the* LORD *gave, and the* LORD *has taken away; blessed be the name of the* LORD.*"[3]

My prayer was born of my faith, yes, but it came easily to my lips because I was stunned. The blow God had struck left me numb. I did not yet feel the pain of my loss; I had not yet plumbed its depth nor had I any idea how long it would endure.

But that was not the end of it. Execrable sores erupted all over my flesh. Even my wife could bear the sight of me no longer. "*Curse God, and die,*"[4] she screamed at me. I have not seen her since.

I took my place with the refuse in the village trash dump. There I sat, scraping at my skin and crying out to a silent God. Life was a burden too heavy to be borne.

> Why did I not die at birth,
>   come forth from the womb and expire?
> Now I would be lying down and quiet;
>   I would be asleep....
> Why is light given to one in misery,
>   and life to the bitter in soul,
> who long for death, but it does not come,
>   and dig for it more than for hidden treasures;
> who rejoice exceedingly,
>   and are glad when they find the grave?[5]

Do you know what I am saying, my friends? Have you ever yearned for the peace of the grave?

Julian: I too have felt life as a heavy weight. I knew much sorrow in my youth. Scarce had I attained the use of reason when the Black Death visited Norwich. What an ugly specter it was! It stalked the streets of our town and without warning struck down whomever it chose. Serf and lord, serving wench and highborn lady, aged crone and mewling infant—none were safe from its scourge.

It began with a sudden fever—not a burning heat, but a kind of deep lethargy that seemed to bode little ill. Within hours, some began to cough and vomit blood; death came swiftly to them. In others, the plague raised swellings—buboes—in the neck or armpit or groin; soon their bodies were covered, like Job's, with horrid boils and purplish blotches. More than half of those thus stricken soon died. Their suffering was dreadful to see.

Among the households the dread specter visited, people fled their closest kin—husband, wife, parent, child—for it seemed that the very breath of the afflicted, even the sight of them, was enough to spread the plague. None could be found to bury the dead for love nor money, so great was the fear that spread in its wake.

When I was thirty and a half, a fever struck me—not the Black Death, but *a bodily sickness in which I lay for three days and three nights; and on the fourth night I received all the rites of Holy Church, and did not expect to live until day. But after this I suffered on for two days and two nights, and on the third night I often thought that I was on the point of death; and those who were around me also thought this....*

I lasted until day, and by then my body was dead from the middle downwards, it felt to me.... After this my sight began to fail, and it was all dark around me in the room, dark as night, except that there was ordinary light trained upon the image of the cross, I never knew how....

After that I felt as if the upper part of my body were beginning to die. My hands fell down on either side, and I was so weak that my head lolled to one side. The greatest pain that I felt was my shortness of breath and the ebbing of my life. Then truly I believed that I was at the point of death. And suddenly in that moment all my pain left me, and I was as sound, particularly in the upper part of my body, as ever I was before or have been since.[6]

And the things I saw then—the Lord's showings to me—I have been pondering all these years. People of your generation, my friends, speak of what happened to me as a near-death experience—seeing a great light, hearing voices, being aware of a loving presence. But not even your science can explain it. Call it what you will, one does not forget such a sight. It changes one forever.

Yet when the visions ended, I soon fell back to myself and to my bodily sickness, understanding that I should live, and as the wretched creature that I am, I grieved and mourned for the bodily pains which I felt, and thought how irksome it was that I must go on living....

I did not believe our Lord God. I believed...truly at the time when I saw him, and it was my will and my intention to do so forever. But like a fool I let it pass from my mind.

See what a wretched creature I am! This was a great sin and a great ingratitude, that I was so foolish, because of a little bodily pain I felt, as to abandon so imprudently the strength of all this blessed revelation from our Lord God.[7]

Hear me, for this was revealed to me and I have come to understand it better over the years: Joy and sorrow are both from God. For those who will not permit themselves to feel their sorrow, those who have encased their hearts in a shell nothing can pierce, cannot know joy. Those who will not feel sorrow cannot allow themselves to feel anything else—not the sweet vulnerability of love, not the tender strivings of hope, not the leap into darkness we call faith.

God wishes us to know that he keeps us safe all the time, in joy and in sorrow, and that he loves us as much in sorrow as in joy.... God gives joy freely as it pleases him, and sometimes he allows us to be in sorrow, and both come from his love. For it is God's will that we do all in our power to preserve our consolation, for bliss lasts forevermore, and pain is passing and will be reduced to nothing.[8]

Job: How fortunate you are to have seen what you saw! God came to comfort you when you had suffered only a few days. Long I sought God's consolation; long I pleaded for some explanation of my misery. I cried out:

> Only grant two things to me,
>   then I will not hide myself from your face:
> withdraw your hand far from me,
>   and do not let dread of you terrify me.
> Then call, and I will answer;
>   or let me speak, and you reply to me....
> Why do you hide your face,
>   and count me as your enemy?[9]

I gave voice to the storm of emotions that shook my soul. I raised my fist to the sky in anger. I lacerated myself for my failure to protect my herds, my servants and my children—most of all, my children!—from the disasters that had overwhelmed me. I groaned beneath the weight of woe that left me near paralyzed.

But God was silent. Have you, companions, also listened to the echoing emptiness of God's silence?

Julian: You did well to speak your pain, Job. Speak it we must, for it is part of who we are. It settles in the very marrow of our bones! We wake with it and sleep with it—or toss sleepless in our beds beneath its weight. The food we eat is bitter with the salt of our tears. Our step is slowed by the burden of sorrow we carry. We cannot wish it away any more than we can wish away the shape of our noses. We cannot escape it; we can only name it and claim it as our own. Until we take our sorrow gently by the hand and befriend it, it remains a bitter foe.

But our pain is not easy to name, for its form shifts and changes like the clouds that scud across the sky of Norwich.

Sometimes pain is like the heavy calm that presages a storm. You see the trees standing strangely still, their leaves untroubled by the slightest breeze. Except for thunderheads building high on the horizon and perhaps a distant rumble, little seems amiss. But the cattle wander from the far corners of the field and gather into a knot; the cat grows restless and circles your ankles. And you know something fierce is afoot.

So it is with sorrow. A blessed numbness descends on your soul and you feel nothing. You go through the motions of arranging a funeral, you hear the doctor's words, you see the ruins of your home or your career. And you watch it all as from a great distance, in the same way you watch the clouds building on the horizon. Everything wears an air of unreality, but you know in your bones something fierce is approaching, and soon the pangs will pierce your soul.

Other storms follow in ragged succession: searing bolts of anger; soul-shaking winds of guilt, blowing in a sense that somehow you are to blame for the disaster; dark, heavy clouds of depression. They sweep across the soul as nature's tantrums sweep a broad plain: rising without warning and often violent in their passing. And just when you think the skies are clearing at last, another tempest strikes. Is that not the climate of sorrow you know, my friends?

There is an end to the season of storms. Blue skies and birdsong, fresh green growth and a deep sense of peace herald a new season of acceptance. But it will not be hurried, any more than the first shoots of spring can be coaxed from the ground in a January blizzard. Before peace dawns, we must turn our faces into the gales and face them squarely. We must learn to pray from feelings we are ashamed of and from no-feeling, or God cannot hear us. For God only hears an honest voice.

Job: My voice was honest! But God did not hear me. God would not answer me. And God was my friend!

I saw the work of God's hands all around me. I saw God's love in the wind that rippled through my fields, in the strength of my oxen, in the smell of bread baking in my wife's oven, in the arms my children clasped about my neck. I saw God's sorrow in the beggars who came to my door, God's hunger for justice in the dealings of commerce. I called God my friend; I spoke my prayers and did my best to act with justice and compassion.

Yet when I spoke my pain, God was silent. When I asked why my Friend had turned away from me, I heard no reply.

Even when at last the voice boomed from the whirlwind, my questions lay unanswered. God gave me only more questions beyond answer. God made me realize more fully what I already knew: I am but a puny mortal before the Power who laid the foundations of the universe and knows its secrets. I am but an incompetent fool before the Wisdom who pastures the beasts and provides for the birds. I am but a helpless worm before the Authority who tames the forces of chaos and brings justice and salvation into human affairs.

My only comfort was that at last God deigned to address me. And I could barely speak.

> I know that you can do all things,
>   and that no purpose of yours can be thwarted.
> "Who is this that hides counsel without
>   knowledge?"

Therefore I have uttered what I did not understand,
things too wonderful for me, which I did not
know.[10]

Julian: Would you had been born into the tradition that has nurtured us! From the earliest ages God spoke to our ancestors in faith. God called Abraham to a new home in a distant land, and promised that childless old man and his aging wife a son and descendants as numerous as the stars in the sky. When the children of Abraham suffered slavery and oppression in the land of the pharaohs, God sent Moses to deliver them.

My Bible tells the story from God's point of view. Wait a minute—ah yes, here it is!

I have observed the misery of my people who are in
Egypt; I have heard their cry on account of their
taskmasters. Indeed, I know their sufferings and I
have come down to deliver them from the
Egyptians, and to bring them up out of that land to a
good and broad land, a land flowing with milk and
honey.... So come, I will send you to Pharaoh to
bring my people, the Israelites, out of Egypt.[11]

And God promised to send his servant, a savior who would triumph over all our pain by taking our suffering upon himself. Excuse me while I thumb. Give me a minute to find the passage I want to read to you. Listen now:

He was despised and rejected by others;
    a man of suffering and acquainted with infirmity;
and as one from whom others hide their faces
    he was despised, and we held him of no account.

Surely he has borne our infirmities

and carried our diseases;
    yet we accounted him stricken,
    struck down by God, and afflicted.

But he was wounded for our transgressions,
    crushed for our iniquities;
upon him was the punishment that made us whole,
    and by his bruises we are healed.[12]

After all these years, I cannot read those words without getting chills. For it was that servant who spoke to me from the cross: Jesus Christ, the Son of God. I saw—no, I felt—his pain. *No tongue may tell, no heart can fully think of the pains which our saviour suffered for us, if we have regard to the honour of him who is the highest, most majestic king, and to his shameful, grievous and painful death. For he who was highest and most honourable was brought low, most utterly despised....*

And suddenly, as I looked at the cross, he changed to an appearance of joy. The change in his appearance changed mine, and I was as glad and joyful as I could possibly be....

Then my Lord put a question to me: Are you well satisfied that I suffered for you? Yes, good Lord, I said.... If you are satisfied, our Lord said, then I am satisfied. It is a joy and a bliss and an endless delight to me that ever I suffered my Passion for you, for if I could suffer more, I would.

...And when he had done it, he would count it all as nothing for love, for everything seems only little to him in comparison with his love.[13]

Indeed, he has suffered much more, and suffers yet, for all that afflicts us is his pain too; even today he weeps with all whose tears scald their faces. He weeps with you, my friends.

And so our good Lord answered to all the questions and doubts which I could raise, saying most comfortingly in this fashion: I will make all things well, I shall make all things well, I may make all things well and I can make all things well; and you will see that yourself, that all things will be well.[14]

I have reflected on those words these many years. I carry them with me into my prayer.

Now it is time to turn to my Psalter. In a moment I will ask you to pray a psalm with me. But first, take a little time to consider some questions.

For Reflection

- *Name your pain: What loss do you face? What emotional storms have swept across your soul?*

- *What kind of storm appears most often on your horizon at the present? How do you express it to God?*

- *Where is your God: near and supportive or silent and distant? How do you—or can you—address this God?*

- *Julian and Job both insist on honesty in prayer. How honest do you dare be with God? Can you speak of anger in prayer?*

- *How easy or hard do you find it to believe with Julian that all will be well? What would help you achieve that belief?*

Closing Prayer

Matthew 27:46 and Mark 15:34 both put the opening words of Psalm 22 on the lips of the dying Jesus. Pray the psalm with him and with your directors. (In a group pray it as a Responsorial Psalm, answering "God, my God, I call on you" after each verse.)

My God, my God, why have you forsaken me?
Why are you so far from helping me, from the
words of my groaning?
O my God, I cry by day, but you do not answer;
and by night, but find no rest....

Yet it was you who took me from the womb;
you kept me safe on my mother's breast.
On you I was cast from my birth,
and since my mother bore me you have been my
God.
Do not be far from me,
for trouble is near
and there is no one to help....

For dogs are all around me;
a company of evildoers encircles me.
My hands and feet have shriveled;
I can count all my bones.
They stare and gloat over me;
they divide my clothes among themselves,
and for my clothing they cast lots.

But you, O LORD, do not be far away!
O my help, come quickly to my aid!
Deliver my soul from the sword,
my life from the power of the dog!
Save me from the mouth of the lion!

...From you comes my praise in the great
congregation;
my vows I will pray before those who fear him.
The poor shall eat and be satisfied;
those who seek him shall praise the LORD.
May your hearts live forever!

All the ends of the earth shall remember
and turn to the LORD;

and all the families of the nations
   shall worship before him.
For dominion belongs to the LORD,
   and he rules over the nations.

To him, indeed, shall all who sleep in the earth
   bow down;
   before him shall bow all who go down to the dust,
   and I shall live for him.
Posterity will serve him; ·
   future generations will be told about the Lord,
and proclaim his deliverance to a people yet unborn,
   saying that he has done it.[15]

Notes

[1] Job 1:21c.

[2] Job 31:16-19, 22.

[3] Job 1:21.

[4] Job 1:9b.

[5] Job 3:11, 13a,b, 20-22.

[6] *Showings*, pp. 127-128.

[7] *Showings*, pp. 162-163.

[8] *Showings*, p. 140.

[9] Job 13:20-22, 24.

[10] Job 42:2-3.

[11] Exodus 3:7b-8c, 10.

[12] Isaiah 53:3-5.

[13] *Showings*, pp. 144-145.

[14] *Showings*, p. 151.

[15] Psalm 22:1-2, 9-11, 16-21, 25-31.

Day Two
Searching for Reasons

Coming Together in the Spirit

On the eve of Yom Kippur, the most solemn and sacred day, an old Jew looked up to heaven and sighed: "Dear God, listen: I, Herschel the tailor, put it to you! The butcher in our village, Shepsel, is a good man, an honorable man, who never cheats anyone and always gives full weight, and who never turns away the needy; yet Shepsel himself is so poor that he and his family sometimes go without meat! ...Or take Fishel, our shoemaker, a model of piety and kindness—yet his beloved mother is dying in terrible pain.... And Reb Label, our *melamed* (teacher), who loves all the lads he teaches and is loved by all who know him, lives hand to mouth, hasn't a decent suit to his name, and just developed an eye disease that may leave him blind! ...So, on this most holy night, I ask You directly, God: Is this *fair*? I repeat: *Is this fair?* ...So, tomorrow, O Lord, on our sacred Yom Kippur—if You forgive us, we will forgive You!"[1]

Defining Our Thematic Context

We, too, have cried out against the unfairness of

suffering—our own and others'—and held God to blame.
Must we forgive God?

In our first session, Julian and Job explored the reality
of human suffering and invited you to name your own
pain. Today they take up the question with which the
author of the Book of Job struggled: Why do people—
especially the innocent—suffer? Let Job and Julian
explore the *why* of suffering with you and see if any of the
answers people commonly put forth satisfy you.

Opening Prayer

Job, stubborn seeker of justice,
be with me in my search for answers.
Lend me your impatience with conventional wisdom,
your faith that God alone has the answers.
Support me with your determination
that God must answer,
that God will hear the cries of the brokenhearted.

Julian, wise counselor,
help me face the questions
that have no answer.
Hear my confusion
and shed light on my path.
Tell me again that,
in spite of explanations that do not satisfy,
all will indeed be well;
every manner of thing will be well.

Wise mentors,
guide me in my search for understanding,
in my search for the God
whom this darkness hides from me.

Retreat Session Two

Job: Did you hear Julian say that my tragedy is not that I was born at all, but that I was born too soon? That my pain would be less had I been nurtured by faith in the God of Moses and his people?

But I am no stranger to that tradition. The one who wrote my story was steeped in it; through him I read the pages of the Hebrew Scriptures. I know of Abraham and Sarah, the aging couple to whom God promised a new land and countless progeny. I know of the God who heard the cries of an oppressed people and led them out of Egypt. I know of the covenant God made with the people of Moses, and the promise Yahweh gave them if they obeyed the commandments:

> ...[A]ll these blessings shall come upon you and overtake you, if you obey the LORD your God:
>
> Blessed shall you be in the city, and blessed shall you be in the field.
>
> Blessed shall be the fruit of your womb, the fruit of your ground, and the fruit of your livestock, both the increase of your cattle and the issue of your flock.
>
> Blessed shall be your basket and your kneading bowl.
>
> Blessed shall you be when you come in, and blessed shall you be when you go out.[2]

The promise rings hollow. For I also know that God sent the obedient Abraham to a mountain in Moriah to sacrifice his son, Isaac, the joy of his old age and the embodiment of the promise. A test, Scripture calls it; it seems a cruel game to me.

This same Yahweh bought one people's freedom at the price of another people's sorrow. The Pharaoh had done evil to the Hebrews, yes, but what about the little people, the powerless of Egypt? The cook in Pharaoh's kitchen, the slave in his fields, the shepherd tending the flock cared not a fig for Pharaoh's building schemes, for his monumental tomb. It was not they who wielded the overseers' whips and goaded the Hebrews to labor under the fierce Egyptian sun until exhaustion felled them. The tears those parents wept over the bodies of their firstborn were doubly bitter.

And where is that God today? Six million people cried out to the God of Moses from the fires of the Holocaust. Six million voices sought God's ear: the voices of bearded old men and brutally ravished young women, the voices of tiny children—beautiful black-eyed babes with numbers tattooed on their arms. Did God hear their cries?

Does that God hear the cries of the children whose corpses float downriver in Rwanda or the little ones whose bellies swell with hunger in the Horn of Africa or the orphaned babes of the disappeared in Latin America? And what about the California child whose parents just last summer tied him in a plastic bag with his feces and left him to suffocate? Did God not hear that tot gasp for breath?

Does God heed the hopelessness of the thousands thrown out of work by plant closings or of the homeless families huddled in a shelter? Does he hear the old woman who wheels through the nursing home halls in search of her family or the homesick stranger whom no co-worker ever invites home for dinner?

> Today also my complaint is bitter;
> his hand is heavy despite my groaning.

Oh, that I knew where I might find him,
   that I might come even to his dwelling!
I would lay my case before him,
   and fill my mouth with arguments.
I would learn what he would answer me,
   and understand what he would say to me.
Would he contend with me in the greatness of his
      power?
No, but he would give heed to me.
There an upright person could reason with him....[3]

Julian: Excuse my tears. I cannot but be moved by the human sorrows Job has sketched for us. He spoke truly when he called himself the voice of all who suffer.

The troubled souls who came to my window raised the same question: Is God deaf to human cries of pain? They came looking for reasons, for the *why* of their sorrow, in the hope that finding some meaning would ease the aching throb of their hearts. *But God forbid that you should say or assume that I am a teacher, for that is not and never was my intention; for I am a woman, ignorant, weak and frail.*[4]

I only know that meaning and reasons are birds of very different feather. Consider two women who came to my window: One's son drowned while saving a child who had tumbled from the pier; the other saw her son hanged for murder. One finds meaning in her son's death; the other only the agony of meaninglessness. Yet both came to me sobbing, recalling their sons as sturdy toddlers, longing to run their hands through their lads' curls just once more.

And neither had reasons. "I raised my son to be gentle and kind," wept the murderer's mother. "Why did someone else not jump in after the child?" sobbed the other. "Why couldn't both man and child have slipped free of the undertow?"

Or consider the plague. The Black Death seemed to slip in the windows as a household slept. Rats were a problem, yes; they spoiled our grain and sometimes bit a baby. Even an anchoress might keep a cat to avoid their unpleasant company. (Pleasant company my cats were, too, purring beside me on my cot!) Fleas were no strangers, either. Every citizen of Norwich, the highborn and the low, scratched a bite from time to time. But we never thought of either as a cause, much less a *reason*, for the sickness that felled so many.

Your age, my friends, has much knowledge. You have named the demon that carries your plague with a name so unpronounceable you call it HIV. You have even named some of its carriers demons. But knowing its cause gives no comfort to the family at the bedside of a wasting son, or offers any reason why it should strike down innocent wives and babies and hemophiliacs.

No, it is not better knowledge that makes better reasons. People of much knowledge and none have been trying to offer explanations for suffering since time immemorial. And all the reasons I have ever heard fall short of comfort. Although each of them may contain a grain of truth, all of them are flawed.

You've heard them all, I'm sure. I know Job has. Shall we risk a look at a few of them?

Job: Why? They are but empty platitudes, religious truisms with no power to comfort.

Julian: Not entirely. They are bits of wisdom painfully gleaned, bits of wisdom hurting people have struggled toward. They are empty of meaning only when they are misused, and they are misused in three ways.

The first is to assume that these truisms, as Job calls

42

them, are the sum of wisdom and can therefore grasp what God is about. For even were they more than tiny scraps of wisdom, God always remains larger, more incomprehensible than we dream.

The second misuse is to force them on people as I would force a nostrum down my cat's throat by holding his muzzle closed until he swallows. For each person's pain is different than anyone else's; each of us has a different history and a different sense of who God is. We must wrestle with our questions ourselves—not alone, mind you, for loneliness only multiplies our anguish. But no answer can truly satisfy us until we have reached it ourselves.

The third misuse—alas, the most common!—is to use truisms to deny the validity of grief, to wish away another's sorrow rather than to share its burden. And that truly is a grievous misuse, for to speak of God without at the same time reflecting God's compassion falsifies the wisest words.

Job: Very well, then. Proceed.

Julian: The first truism, of course, is that we *deserve* whatever happens to us, that we suffer because we are sinful.

Job: Once I was certain that the just prosper and the wicked are brought low. My own life was a case in point: I walked in the way of God as best I understood it. And great wealth and happiness were mine

> because I delivered the poor who cried,
>   and the orphan who had no helper.
> The blessing of the wretched came upon me,
>   and I caused the widow's heart to sing for joy.

I put on righteousness, and it clothed me;
　　my justice was like a robe and a turban.
I was eyes to the blind,
　　and feet to the lame.
I was a father to the needy,
　　and I championed the cause of the stranger.
I broke the fangs of the unrighteous,
　　and made them drop their prey from their teeth.
Then I thought, I shall die in my nest,
　　and I shall multiply my days like the phoenix....[5]

And then my happiness crumbled to dust and I was sore afflicted. My friends told me at great and tiring length that my protestation of innocence was a lie. Surely I had offended God to be brought so low! That argument persuades me not at all.

I hold fast my righteousness, and will not let it go;
　　my heart does not reproach me for any of my
　　　　days.[6]

What do you think, my friends? Was I not right to stand firm in my innocence? Surely you are no more deserving of your pain than I was.

　　Further, God *destroys both the blameless and the wicked*[7]—indeed, smites the just and leaves the wicked untouched.

Why do the wicked live on,
　　reach old age, and grow mighty in power?
Their children are established in their presence,
　　and their offspring before their eyes.
Their houses are safe from fear,
　　and no rod of God is upon them....
They spend their days in prosperity,
　　and in peace they go down to Sheol.[8]

Julian: But people offer another explanation that touches Job's story: Suffering is God's way of testing us.

Job: You mean the wager between God and the satan? Only those who are ignorant of the uses of story—those who call me fiction—could take that exchange literally. It is only a way to pose a question: Is it possible to love God for God's sake, or do humans worship and lead good lives only because they expect some return from God?

If you still wish to believe the framework the ancient author used is fact, look at the story's end:

> And the LORD restored the fortunes of Job.... The LORD blessed the latter days of Job more than his beginning; and he had fourteen thousand sheep, six thousand camels, a thousand yoke of oxen, and a thousand donkeys. He also had seven sons and three daughters.... In all the land there were no women so beautiful as Job's daughters....[9]

Do you think twenty strong sons could replace the seven I lost? A hundred beautiful daughters could not take the place of even one—the youngest, my merry, dimpled Leah! How could I enjoy wealth with the ease I once knew when I know how quickly it can disappear? Do you think I have no feeling for the servants who died tending my sheep and camels? And my wife—what deep scars would remain between us!

But what about Abraham? Your own Scriptures speak of a test in his case. ·

Julian: You ask me to read your story with care, yet you would handle the Bible that is my daily companion so carelessly! Wiser heads than mine study our Scriptures.

They say that Abraham's trip to Moriah is also an author's way of raising a question: Does God take pleasure in the child sacrifice practiced by Abraham's neighbors in his new home? And the answer is a resounding "No!"

I know a woman of your time, my friends, who was to read the account of Abraham's journey to Moriah with Isaac at liturgy one Sunday morning. Waiting for her in the sacristy was an introduction prepared by her parish worship commission explaining God's rejection of child sacrifice. Also there she learned of the news that was sweeping through the assembling worshipers like fire through dry brush: A daughter of the parish, a lovely red-haired seventeen-year-old, had died in the small hours of that morning in an automobile accident. Without the introduction, what message would the listeners have heard in God's word? "Take your sons and daughters, the beautiful young people who carry your hopes and dreams, and send them out on the roads where drunken drivers swerve"? "Weep not for this young woman nor for her parents; this is only a test"?

No, a good teacher does not spring the test before presenting the lesson. Surely God is a good teacher!

Job: I have heard it said that suffering itself is the lesson, that it purifies us as the furnace purifies gold and teaches us such fine things as humility, patience and compassion. Yet when I saw a parent hold a toddler's hand to the fire to teach the tot that fire burns, I thought it cruel.

Julian: I think it cruel; don't you, dear friends?

In my youth I held to the belief that suffering teaches. I had *a desire of my will to have by God's grace a bodily sickness. I wished that sickness to be so severe that it might seem mortal.... I wanted to have every kind of pain, bodily and*

spiritual, which I should have if I died, every fear and
temptation from devils, and every other kind of pain except the
departure of the spirit. I intended this because I wanted to be
purged by God's mercy, and afterwards live more to his
glory....[10]
But now I see that suffering itself is not enough. Some
people do emerge from the crucible of pain stronger,
wiser, gentler. But others emerge embittered and hateful.
A young mother grieving the murder of her little son
heard that answer and refuted it:

> I do not believe that sheer suffering teaches. If
> suffering taught, all the world would be wise, since
> everyone suffers. To suffering must be added
> mourning, understanding, patience, love, openness,
> and the willingness to remain vulnerable. All these
> and other factors combined, if the circumstances are
> right, *can* teach and *can* lead to rebirth.[11]

That woman belonged to your time. Her name was Anne
Morrow Lindbergh. Although she wrote those words in
her diary when her grief was raw and new, she did
indeed achieve wholeness. She later shared her hard-
gained wisdom in her writings.

What the Lord showed to me was this: *I saw a merciful*
compassion which our Lord has for us because of our woe, and
a courteous promise of a clean deliverance, for he wants us to be
comforted in surpassing joy.[12]

And so our good Lord answered to all the questions and
doubts which I could raise, saying most comfortingly: I may
make all things well, and I will make all things well, and I shall
make all things well, and you will see yourself that every kind
of thing will be well.[13]

Job: That smacks of another story I have heard before:

that God has a grand design in mind, and our sufferings are included in the plan.

A writer of our friends' century—a novelist named Thornton Wilder—lays our lack of understanding to the limits of our view in a pretty image. His rationale has grown dear to preachers' hearts: God is stitching a tapestry, a work of delicate shadings and great beauty. But only God sees it from the right side. We who look up at the underside can see only a tangle of threads, loose ends and knots.

Julian: The tangles are of our own making; we are the knots. God's grand design is simply this: that we love God and one another. But when he told me that all will be well, *I stood, contemplating it generally, darkly and mournfully, saying...with very great fear: Ah, good Lord, how could all things be well, because of the great harm which has come through sin to your creatures? ...And to this our blessed Lord answered, very meekly and with a most loving manner, and he showed me that Adam's sin was the greatest harm ever done or ever to be done until the end of the world. And he also showed me that this is plainly known to all Holy Church upon earth.*[14]

Job: How can one man's sin—or one couple's—be responsible for all the suffering in the world? Hasn't each of you sometimes wondered if God is so vengeful as to curse all of humanity for one sin? Yet your own prophets refute that idea:

> The word of the LORD came to me: What do you mean by repeating this proverb concerning the land of Israel, "The parents have eaten sour grapes, and the children's teeth are set on edge"? As I live, this proverb shall no more be used by you in Israel.

Know that all lives are mine; the life of the parent as well as the life of the child is mine; it is only the person who sins that shall die.[15]

Julian: But consider the nature of Adam's sin. He and Eve ate the fruit not of any tree, but of the only one forbidden to them: the tree that gave knowledge of good and evil. Once something is known, it cannot become once again unknown. Once humanity lost its innocence, it could not again return to the blissful ignorance the beasts know.

A dog will lie on its mistress' grave, patiently waiting for her return, for the poor dumb thing has no knowledge of death's finality. But her husband and her children know. Her little ones cry in the night for the comfort of their mother's arms. Their father has no consolation to give, for his own heart is breaking.

A deer, mortally wounded by the hunter's weapon, will seek out a quiet corner of the forest, lie down and die without questioning the justice of its wound. But we know that death stalks us. We fear the plague, the fire in the thatched roof, the knife in the darkened alley. We fear because we know that everything we fear will come to pass.

It says here in my Bible:

As for mortals, their days are like grass;
   they flourish like a flower of the field;
for the wind passes over it, and it is gone,
   and its place knows it no more.[16]

Job: Then I was right: All these words are but empty platitudes.

My days are swifter than the weaver's shuttle,

and come to their end without hope.[17]

Julian: Not so—not without hope! Trust me, my
friends—not without hope! When the Lord told me *that
Adam's sin was the greatest harm ever done or ever to be done
until the end of the world...* he also said, *For since I have set
right the greatest of harms, then it is my will that you should
know through this that I shall set right everything which is
less.*[18]

Do you not think it strange that all the reasons offered
to explain our anguish assign our misfortunes to God's
will? It brings to my mind something I saw on a modern
miracle, television.

A talk show host once put this question to the guests:
"How often did your mother tell you she loved you?"
Watching the show was a woman who had suffered much
abuse at her mother's hands. An unbidden thought
popped into her head: "Whenever she was going to hurt
me. Again and again she said, 'I'm only doing this
because I love you.'"

Just so, when we speak of God's will—God who is our
loving Father and Mother!—we usually mean something
painful. Never do we cite God's will when the sunset
paints the sky with radiant splendor, when the trees burst
into springtime blossoms, when love delights us and joy
finds us. Yet *it is God's will that we know he has not forgotten
us. And this is what he means and says for comfort in these
words: And you will never again have pain of any kind, any
kind of sickness, any kind of displeasure, any lack of your will,
but always joy and bliss without end.*[19]

Surely we need to discover this God who loves us so
tenderly. *God wishes to be seen, and he wishes to be sought,
and he wishes to be expected, and he wishes to be trusted.*[20]

But that is a task for another day. Now the shadows
grow long outside my window. It is time for reflection,

for prayer and for rest.

For Reflection

- *Do you agree with Job and Julian that the reasons for human suffering they put forth are empty of comfort? Why or why not?*

- *What other explanations have you heard? Which, if any, has brought you lasting consolation?*

- *If you could face God in court, how would you present your case? What questions would you put to God?*

- *Do you think God sends pain and sorrow into your life? How does that affect your feelings about God?*

- *What good things come to your mind when you speak of God's will?*

Closing Prayer

(Group response: "Deliver me, O God.")

O LORD, do not rebuke me in your anger,
    or discipline me in your wrath.
Be gracious to me, O LORD, for I am languishing;
    O LORD, heal me, for my bones are shaking with
        terror.
My soul also is struck with terror,
    while you, O LORD—how long?

Turn, O LORD, save my life;
    deliver me for the sake of your steadfast love.
For in death there is no remembrance of you;
    in Sheol who can give you praise?

I am weary with my moaning;
    every night I flood my bed with tears;
    I drench my couch with my weeping.
My eyes waste away because of grief;
    they grow weak because of all my foes.

Depart from me, all you workers of evil,
    for the LORD has heard the sound of my weeping.
The LORD has heard my supplication;
    the LORD accepts my prayer.
All my enemies shall be ashamed and struck with
    terror;
    they shall turn back, and in a moment be put to
    shame.[21]

Notes

[1] *The Joys of Yiddish*, by Leo Rosten (New York: McGraw-Hill Book Company, 1968), p. 4.

[2] Deuteronomy 28:2-18

[3] Job 23:2-7a.

[4] *Showings*, p. 135.

[5] Job 29:12-18.

[6] Job 27:6.

[7] Job 9:22b.

[8] Job 21:7-9, 13.

[9] Job 42:10a, 12-13, 15a.

[10] *Showings*, p. 178.

[11] *Hour of Gold, Hour of Lead*, by Anne Morrow Lindbergh (New York: Harcourt Brace Jovanovich, Inc., 1973), pp. 179-180.

[12] *Showings*, p. 307.

[13] *Showings*, p. 229.

[14] *Showings*, pp. 227-228.

[15] Ezekiel 18:1-4.

[16] Psalm 103:15-16.

[17] Job 7:6.

[18] *Showings*, p. 228.

[19] *Showings*, p. 307.

[20] *Showings*, p. 194.

[21] Psalm 6.

DAY THREE
Searching for God

Coming Together in the Spirit

The pueblo peoples of the Southwest, the Hopi and the Zuñi, honor sacred beings called *kachinas*. These lesser deities, they believe, once walked the earth; they are the spirits of departed ancestors. Every year the kachinas return to earth for six months, bringing with them hhe rainclouds so precious to a desert people.

The tribal priests, robed in colorful costumes and elaborate masks, honor the kachinas in a ceremonial dance. When the rites are over, the masks are carefully hidden away, for the children are taught that the dancers are the real kachinas, who will punish or reward them as their behavior merits.

When the children reach the brink of adulthood, a solemn initiation ceremony occurs. The kachina priests, after appropriate ritual, suddenly remove their masks, revealing their true identities to the horrified children.

Thus the youngsters are launched on a search for a new, adult understanding of the supernatural.

Defining Our Thematic Context

Suffering shakes our world; it can shatter our concept

of God and launch us on a search for better understanding of who God is for us. The vision of God underlying the arguments put forth by Job's friends has deep biblical roots. In that view (called Deuteronomist by Scripture scholars after the biblical author who set it forth), God acts strictly out of justice. Divine blessings rest firmly on the condition Moses set forth:

> See, I am setting before you today a blessing and a curse: the blessing, *if* you obey the commandments of the LORD your God that I am commanding you today; and the curse, *if* you do not obey the commandments of the LORD your God....[1]

This is the view of God that the ancient author set out to refute in Job's story. Yet it endures among believers even today.

Another vision of God persistently threads its way through Scripture: the God whose love is given freely and firmly without condition. This is the God who promised David a lasting throne and a descendant who would rule forever (see 2 Samuel 7:1-16, on which Israel based its hope for the Messiah). This is the God of whose faithful love Isaiah sang:

> Can a woman forget her nursing child,
>   or show no compassion for the child of her womb?
> Even these may forget,
>   yet I will not forget you.[2]

Today Job and Julian profess their faith in the God whose love endures. Let them walk with you on your search for this God.

Opening Prayer

Job, faithful believer,
guide my steps toward the God who befriends us.
Lend me your certainty that God cares,
your faith that God hears the cry of the needy.
Support me with your determination
to insist that God be spoken of truly,
to seek a loving God.

Julian, sweet visionary,
help me see the God you saw,
to find healing in the tenderness
of the divine gaze.
Guide my search for the God who comforts.
Tell me again that God
can make all things well,
will make all things well,
that I will see for myself
that every manner of thing will be well.

Wise mentors,
guide me in my search for the God
whose love will bring light
to the darkness that surrounds me.

RETREAT SESSION THREE

Job: In my sorrow I sought God to no avail. I wept for want of God's presence:

If I go forward he is not there;
   or backward, I cannot perceive him;
on the left he hides, and I cannot behold him;
   I turn to the right, but I cannot see him.[3]

Yet I believe that God seeks us even before we set out on our search. I glimpsed God's beauty in the wonder of creation; I saw God's will when people treated one another with justice and compassion. I sensed God's very being in the miracle of birth, in the magical surprise of being loved, in my children's bright eyes and bubbling laughter.

Julian: Yes, and even in the mystery of suffering and death.

Job: You speak the truth! My afflictions set me off on a search for a new and deeper understanding of God, just as our friends here have come seeking our company on their quest—isn't that so? And finally, at the end of my search, I saw the God I sought with my own eyes. And what I saw so far surpassed the feeble "wisdom" my friends offered that I could speak no more.

Julian: Just so does God reach out to us. My showings *taught me to understand that the soul's constant search pleases God greatly. For it cannot do more than seek, suffer and trust.... Seeking with faith, hope and love pleases our Lord, and finding pleases the soul and fills it full of joy. And so I was taught to understand that seeking is as good as contemplating.... It is God's will that we seek until we see him, for it is through this that he will show himself to us, of his special grace, when it is his will.*[4]
   If God wishes to show you more, he will be your light; you need none but him. For I saw him and sought him, for we are

now so blind and foolish that we can never seek God until the time when he in his goodness shows himself to us. And when by grace we see something of him, then we are moved to seek with greater desire to see him for our greater joy. So I saw him and sought him, and I had him and lacked him; and this is and should be our ordinary undertaking in this life as I see it.... For it is God's will that we believe that we see him continually, though it seems to us that the sight be only partial; and through this belief he makes us always to gain more grace....[5]

Job: I saw myself clearly, too: I saw that I had tried to force God to behave according to my understanding no less than my friends had. They had insisted God must punish the wicked; I had demanded that God reward the virtuous—or, at least, explain to me why such disaster had overtaken me. Haven't you made the same demand, friends?

As another poet who told my story, one Archibald MacLeish, put it, I wanted justice, when love is all there is. I saw my sin well, *therefore I despise myself,/ and repent in dust and ashes.*[6]

Julian: It is all a part of Adam's sin. He wanted to be like God; he wanted to deny the impassable distance between God's being and ours. The same temptation besets us. And one form it takes is the refusal to let God be God, to remake God in our own image. But we cannot know ourselves until we know God, until we see our littleness before God. *For our soul sits in God in true rest, and our soul stands in God in sure strength, and our soul is naturally rooted in God in endless love. And therefore if we want to have knowledge of our soul and communion and discourse with it, we must seek in our Lord God in whom it is enclosed.*[7]

Please do not misunderstand me, my friends. I do not mean to say that God is all-powerful and can destroy us with no more thought than I take when I step on a bug that has invaded my cell. Let me tell you what God showed to me about our littleness, for it was wondrous to behold.

I saw that he is everything which is good and comforting for our help. He is our clothing, who wraps and enfolds us for love, embraces and shelters us, surrounds us for his love, which is so tender that he may never desert us....

And in this he showed me something small, no bigger than a hazelnut, lying in the palm of my hand, and it was round as a ball. I looked at it with the eye of my understanding and thought: What can this be? I was amazed that it could last, for I thought that because of its littleness it would suddenly have fallen into nothing. And I was answered in my understanding: It lasts and always will, because God loves it; and thus everything has being through the love of God. In this little thing I saw three properties. The first is that God made it, the second is that God loves it, the third is that God preserves it. But what did I see in it? It is that God is the Creator and the protector and the lover.[8]

But the reason why it seemed to my eyes so little was because I saw it in the presence of him who is the Creator. For to a soul who sees the Creator of all things, all that is created seems very little.[9]

Job: So be it! What surprised me when I saw myself before God was that God spoke well of me in spite of my sin. He demanded that my friends ask my prayers— mine!—for forgiveness because, God told them, *you have not spoken of me what is right, as my servant Job has.*[10]

Another poet who retold my story, Robert Frost, brought God back to visit me in my restored prosperity and amplified those words:

I've had you on my mind for a thousand years

To thank you someday for the way you helped me
Establish once and for all the principle
There's no connection man can reason out
Between his just deserts and what he gets....
Too long I've owed you this apology
For the apparently unmeaning sorrow
You were afflicted with in those old days.
....I have no doubt
You realize by now the part you played
To stultify the Deuteronomist
And change the tenor of religious thought.
My thanks are to you for releasing me
From moral bondage to the human race.
The only free will there at first was man's,
Who could do good or evil as he chose.
I had no choice but to follow him
With forfeits and rewards he understood—
Unless I liked to suffer loss of worship.
I had to prosper good and punish evil.
You changed all that. You set me free to reign.[11]

Julian: Yet many people—myself among them, and
surely you, my friends—ask why, if God reigns, sin and
suffering are allowed a place in the world. *In this naked
word "sin," our Lord brought generally to my mind all which
is not good, and the shameful contempt and the direst
tribulation which he endured for us in this life, and his death
and all his pains, and the passions, spiritual and bodily, of all
his creatures. For we are all in part troubled, and we shall be
troubled, following our master Jesus until we are fully purged
of our mortal flesh and all our inward affections which are not
very good....*

*But I did not see sin, for I believe that it has no kind of
substance, no share in being, nor can it be recognized except by
the pain caused by it. And it seems to me that this pain is
something for a time, for it purges and makes us know*

ourselves and ask for mercy.... And because of the tender love which our good Lord has for all who will be saved, he comforts readily and sweetly, meaning this: It is true that sin is the cause of all this pain, but all will be well, and every kind of thing will be well.[12]

Job: Sin has no kind of substance? How can that be, when sinful human beings inflict such pain on one another? Sin seems very real to me!

Julian: It has no substance, no share in being, because it lacks the three properties of God's creation. God did not make it; God does not love it; God does not preserve it. *I saw hidden in God an exalted and wonderful mystery, which he will make plain and we shall know in heaven. In this knowledge we shall truly see the cause why he allowed sin to come, and in this sight we shall rejoice forever.*[13]

Job: But surely the belief my friends held was not without truth: Sin does anger God.

Julian: *I saw no kind of wrath in God, neither briefly nor for very long. For truly, as I see it, if God could be angry for any time, we should have neither life nor place nor being; for as truly as we have our being from the endless power of God and from his endless wisdom and from his endless goodness, just as truly we have our preservation in the endless power of God and in his endless wisdom and in his endless goodness. For though we may feel in ourselves anger, contention and strife, still we are all mercifully enclosed in God's mildness and in his meekness, in his benignity and in his accessibility.*[14]

Israel used a lovely word to describe God's courteous kindness: *hesed.* It expresses God's very essence: kind and merciful, slow to anger and abounding in steadfast love and faithfulness. Saint John put it more simply: "God is love, and those who abide in love abide in God, and God in them."[15]

This is the God of whom the evangelist says, "For God so loved the world that he gave his only Son.... Indeed, God did not send the Son into the world to condemn it, but in order that the world might be saved through him."[16]

Job: The fact remains that, as Frost said, there is no connection between our just deserts and what we get. Great pain afflicts those who treat all creation gently no less than it afflicts those who inflict suffering on others. It is as though God has chosen to be helpless, to stand outside the world and watch us perish in misery. Hasn't that thought crossed your mind, my friends?

Julian: I asked that question. *And to this I had no other answer as a revelation from our Lord except this: What is impossible to you is not impossible to me. I shall preserve my word in everything, and I shall make everything well.*[17] God does not stand by in helplessness; God acts in ways we cannot grasp. Let me turn to my Bible again. The prophet Isaiah says:

> For my thoughts are not your thoughts,
>   nor are your ways my ways, says the LORD.
> For as the heavens are higher than the earth,
>   so are my ways higher than your ways
>   and my thoughts than your thoughts.[18]

Yet one thing I know: The God who has given us the freedom to sin has also given us the freedom to seek signs of divine love within our world. Better yet, we have the power to make—to be—such signs. We must explore that possibility another day.

It is known that before miracles come sorrows and anguish
and trouble, and that because we ought to know our own
weakness and the harm we have fallen into through sin, to
humble us and make us cry to God for help and grace. And
afterwards great miracles come, and that is from God's great
power and wisdom and goodness, showing his might and the
joys of heaven, so much as this may be in this passing life, and
that is for the strengthening of our faith, and as this may
increase our hope in love.[19]

Job: God does work such wonders. They happen daily in
today's hospitals, where skilled hands lift the cloud of
cataracts from aging eyes and reattach severed fingers—
even set a dead man's heart beating in another's chest!

They happen without human intervention, as well.
The archives at Lourdes hold evidence not only of a
malignancy's disappearance but also of cancer-ridden
bone restored to wholeness. Deadly diseases suddenly go
into remission, leaving physicians to shake their heads in
awe. A plane falls from the sky and spreads shattered
pieces of metal and flesh, and one person walks away
shaken but unharmed.

When bad news crashes into our lives, our first
reaction is to disbelieve it. "It can't be true," we protest.
"Please, don't let it be!" When the messengers of doom
came running to me one after another, I too prayed, "O
God, let it not be true!" But it *was* true, all of it—my flocks
and herds, my servants and oh! my children were gone. I
did not ask God to undo it; that seemed too much to ask
even of God. But when the boils erupted, I was too
broken to ask for healing. Instead, I sought an
explanation.

Yet people do seek healing—first from the doctors and
then, when that fails, from God. Why don't miracles
happen more often? Is it, as some say, that we don't pray

hard enough, or that we don't have enough faith?

Julian: I think not. Were miraculous healings the rule rather than the exception, they would have little power to move us to deeper faith. And they would so overshadow the everyday miracles we witness—the birth of a child, the swelling buds of springtime, the unexpected kindness of a stranger, the love that carries a man and a woman together into old age—that we would fail to see how good and how dear God's creation is.

You spoke of Lourdes and the great wonders which have occurred there. Know you not that physical healings are rare even in such a blessed spot? Yet people come away healed in spirit if not in body, carrying with them a sense of deep trust and peace. Surely a broken heart made whole is one of God's wondrous works! Would you not think it so, my friends?

But God holds many wonders in store for us. *There is a deed which the blessed Trinity will perform on the last day, as I see it, and what the deed will be and how it will be performed is unknown to every creature who is inferior to Christ, and it will be until the deed is done.... This is the great deed ordained by our Lord God without beginning, treasured and hidden in his blessed breast, known only to himself, through which deed he will make all things well. For just as the blessed Trinity created all things from nothing, just so will the same Trinity make everything well which is not well.*[20]

My Bible hints at it. Listen:

> Then I saw a new heaven and a new earth; for the
> first heaven and the first earth had passed away,
> and the sea was no more.... And I heard a loud voice
> from the throne saying,
>> "See, the home of God is among mortals.
>> He will dwell with them as their God;

they will be his peoples,
and God himself will be with them;
he will wipe every tear from their eyes.
Death will be no more;
mourning and crying and pain will be no more,
for the first things have passed away."
And the one who was seated on the throne said,
"See, I am making all things new."[21]

Job: Had I half the patience ascribed to me by people who have never read my story through, I could have waited in peace for God to do this great deed. But my soul, as well you know, has yet to know the serenity in which yours rests—and we are speaking, in my case, of many centuries!

Julian: But we need not wait. God's miracles, the signs of God's nearness and care, surround us even now. And the great deed God will do *will be begun here, and it will be honour to God and to the plentiful profit of all his lovers on earth; and as we come to heaven each one of us will see it with wonderful joy; and it will go on operating until the last day.*[22]

For our blessed Lord yearns even now to comfort us. It is his will and pleasure that we be well and happy, just as it is a mother's will and pleasure that her child be well and happy.

This fair lovely word "mother" is so sweet and so kind in itself that it cannot be truly said of anyone or to anyone except of him and to him who is the true Mother of life and of all things. To the property of motherhood belong nature, love, wisdom and knowledge, and this is God.... The kind, loving mother who knows and sees the need of her child guards it very tenderly, as the nature and condition of motherhood will have. And always, as the child grows in age and in stature, she acts differently, but she does not change her love. And when it is older, she allows it to be chastised to destroy its faults, so as to make the child receive virtues and grace. This work, with everything which is lovely and good, our Lord performs.... So he is our Mother in nature by the operation of grace for the lower part, for love of the higher part. And he wants us to know it, for he wants to have all our love attached to him....[23]

Job: I remember my mother's tenderness, her pride in my accomplishments, the delight she took in her grandchildren. And I loved to watch my wife with our little ones. When they were small, she spoiled them shamelessly. "There are two kinds of spoiling," she'd tell me, "the good kind and the bad kind. And the good kind is every child's birthright."

Julian: Just so does God mother us. Like newborn babes, we are frail creatures who would fall into nothing without God's love. Infants know their need; they cling to their mothers for their very lives. We have barely begun to grasp our need. Tomorrow we can talk about our frailty. But now I am weary and you must be, too. Let us rest well tonight, securely enfolded in our Mother's love. But first, let us reflect and then turn to the Psalter.

For Reflection

- *What indications of God's love have you glimpsed?*

- *What do you think of when someone speaks of "God's will"?*

- *How has your concept of God changed over the course of your lifetime? How has suffering caused you to rethink your understanding of God?*

- *What do you believe about miracles? Can you bring yourself to ask God to undo what is done? Why or why not?*

- *Is* mother *one of the words you would use to describe God? Why or why not?*

Closing Prayer

(Group response: "Great is your steadfast love.")

Incline your ear, O Lord, and answer me,
    for I am poor and needy.
Preserve my life, for I am devoted to you;
    save your servant who trusts in you.
You are my God; be gracious to me, O Lord,
    for to you do I cry all day long.

Gladden the soul of your servant,
    for to you, O Lord, I lift up my soul.
For you, O Lord, are good and forgiving,
    abounding in steadfast love to all who call on you.

Give ear, O Lord, to my prayer;
    listen to my cry of supplication.
In the day of my trouble I call on you,
    for you will answer me.

O God, the insolent rise up against me;
    a band of ruffians seeks my life,
    and they do not set you before them.
But you, O Lord, are a God merciful and gracious,
    slow to anger and abounding in steadfast love and
        faithfulness.

Turn to me and be gracious to me;
    give your strength to your servant;
    save the child of your serving girl.

Show me a sign of your favor,
   so that those who hate me may see it and be put to
   shame,
   because you, LORD, have helped me and
   comforted me.[24]

Notes

[1] Deuteronomy 11:26-28a, emphasis added.

[2] Isaiah 49:15.

[3] Job 23:8-9.

[4] *Showings*, p. 195.

[5] *Showings*, p. 193-194.

[6] Job 42:6.

[7] *Showings*, p. 289.

[8] *Showings*, p. 183.

[9] *Showings*, p. 133.

[10] Job 42:7c.

[11] *A Masque of Reason*, by Robert Frost. *The Poetry of Robert Frost*, edited by Edward Connery Lathem (New York: Holt, Rinehart and Winston, 1969), pp. 475-476.

[12] *Showings*, p. 225.

[13] *Showings*, p. 226.

[14] *Showings*, p. 264.

[15] 1 John 4:16b.

[16] John 3:16a, 17.

[17] *Showings*, p. 233.

[18] Isaiah 55:8-9.

[19] *Showings*, pp. 240-241.

[20] *Showings*, pp. 232-233.

[21] Revelation 21:1, 3-5a.

[22] *Showings*, p. 238.

[23] *Showings*, pp. 298-299.

[24] Psalm 86:1-7, 14-17.

DAY FOUR
Embracing Brokenness

Coming Together in the Spirit

After Adam and Eve had been banished from the Garden of Eden, God saw that they were penitent and took their fall very much to heart. And as He is a Compassionate Father, He said to them gently: "Unfortunate children! I have punished you for your sin and have driven you out of the Garden of Eden where you were living without care and in great well-being. Now you are about to enter into a world of sorrow and trouble the like of which staggers the imagination. However, I want you to know that My benevolence and My love for you will never end. I know that you will meet with a lot of tribulation in the world and that it will embitter your lives. For that reason I give you out of my heavenly treasure this priceless pearl. Look! It is a tear! And when grief overtakes you and your heart aches so that you are not able to endure it, and great anguish grips your soul, then there will fall from your eyes this tiny tear. Your burden will grow lighter then."

When Adam and Eve heard these words sorrow overcame them. Tears welled up in their eyes, rolled down their cheeks and fell to earth.

And it was these tears of anguish that first

moistened the earth. Adam and Eve left them as a precious inheritance to their children. And since then, whenever a human being is in great trouble and his heart aches and his spirit is oppressed then the tears begin to flow from his eyes and lo! the gloom is lifted.[1]

Defining Our Thematic Context

In our last session, Julian spoke of a God who holds everything that is made in loving hands, of a God who embraces us as tenderly as a mother cradles her infant. Yet in the first few days of life, infants wail without tears. As we become more familiar with fear and pain, the gift God gave Adam and Eve begins to spill down our cheeks.

We grow up, and forget the pain of infant helplessness; we acquire coping skills and grow in self-confidence. In the flood of tears that accompanies suffering, our confidence is swept away, and we begin to discover the truth about ourselves: We are indeed as helpless as a newborn child.

Today Julian and Job look at the brokenness that is the human condition. Let them help you claim your place among the wounded and see your tears as a gift from God.

Opening Prayer

> Job, stubborn supplicant,
> make room for me on your trash dump.
> Lend me your refusal to be one more shard of broken
>   pottery,
> your insistence that God must reach down to you

and lift you up in loving hands.
Support me with your willingness
to persevere in prayer,
to demand that the God who made us
must in love sustain us
or we perish.

Julian, wise observer,
you saw in the pain-racked who came to your
    window
the sad condition of our kind,
and you spoke of God's care.
Help me come to terms with my helplessness,
with my brokenness.
Speak to me of the God who formed us,
of God's dreams for our happiness,
of God's yearning to make all things well.
Remind me once more
that every manner of thing will be well.

Wise mentors,
teach me wisdom and patience with myself.
Show me that my wounds
run even deeper than I know,
and lead me to the Divine Physician.

Retreat Session Four

Job: I said that I dared not ask God to undo what was
done, yet that is what I wished were possible!

Oh, that I were as in the months of old,
  as in the days when God watched over me;
when his lamp shone over my head,
  and by his light I walked through darkness;
when I was in my prime,
  when the friendship of God was upon my tent;
when the Almighty was still with me,
  when my children were around me;
when my steps were washed with milk,
  and the rock poured out for me streams of oil![2]

Haven't you also yearned to see the past rewritten, friends?

Julian: Your grief is your friend, Job—and so is yours, my friends. For it allows you to mourn. And there is reason to mourn, for we are broken creatures—like the little sparrow that once found its way into my cell. The wee thing fluttered its wings in terror and sought its freedom. But before I could say an *Ave* my cat had it in his claws.

Poor cat! I laid such a fright on him that he tore under my cot to sulk out the day. I could not blame him: He is a hunter by nature—and I bless him for it every time he lays a mouse or rat at my feet. Surely the God who made the sparrow and watches it with such a loving eye also made the cats, great and small, and delights in their lithe skill.

But my screams came late for the sparrow. The little bird's wing was broken. I sent it home with my maidservant to tend at a safe distance from Puss. Its wing mended, she told me, but badly; it could fly only in little fluttering hops. That, I thought, was very sad.

The swans in the castle moat, I hear, have been deliberately maimed so that they cannot fly away, and that is sadder still, for it is cruel. But God did not clip our wings. God made us to soar to the highest heavens, but we cannot *because our spiritual eye is so blind, and we are so burdened with the weight of our mortal flesh and the darkness of sin that we cannot see clearly the blessed face of the Lord our God. No, and because of this darkness, we can scarcely believe or have faith in his great love and his faithfulness, with which he protects us. And so it is I say that we can never cease mourning and weeping....*[3]

Job: So we do.

> A mortal, born of woman, few of days and full of
>   trouble,
>   comes up like a flower and withers,
>   flees like a shadow and does not last....
>
> For there is hope for a tree,
>   if it is cut down, that it will sprout again,
>   and that its shoots will not cease.
> Though its root grows old in the earth,
>   and its stump dies in the ground,
> yet at the scent of water it will bud
>   and put forth branches like a young plant.
> But mortals die, and are laid low;
>   humans expire, and where are they?[4]

Julian: As safe in God's hands as the sparrow in mine! For God is a tender lord who cares for the sparrow's broken wing. Remember that there is matter for mirth as well as for mourning—*matter for mirth, that the Lord, our maker is so near to us and in us, and we in him, because of his great goodness he keeps us faithfully....*[5]

And if we were in all the pain that heart can think or tongue can tell, if we could at that time see his blessed face, all this pain would not grieve us...

We ought to have three kinds of knowledge. The first is that we know our Lord God. The second is that we know ourselves, what we are through him in nature and in grace. The third is that we know humbly that ourself is opposed to our sin and to our weakness.[6]

It is necessary *to see and know that we are sinners and commit many evil deeds which we ought to forsake, and leave many good deeds undone which we ought to do....*[7] All of us can say with Saint Paul:

> I do not understand my own actions. For I do not do what I want, but I do the very thing I hate.... For I do not do the good I want, but the evil I do not want is what I do. Now if I do what I do not want, it is no longer I that do it, but sin that dwells within me.... For I delight in the law of God in my inmost self, but I see in my members another law at war with the law of my mind, making me captive to the law of sin that dwells in my members. Wretched man that I am! Who will rescue me from this body of death?[8]

Job: And will we never fly but in fluttering hops? Will we always bear the wound of sin, and with it the wounds that life inflicts upon us?

Julian: A rabbi, our friends' contemporary, tells this story:

> There is an old Chinese tale about the woman whose only son died. In her grief she went to the holy man and said, "What prayers, what magical incantations do you have to bring my son back to life?" Instead of sending her away or reasoning with her, he said to her, "Fetch me a mustard seed from a home that has never known sorrow. We will use it to drive the sorrow out of your life." The woman set off at once in search of that magical mustard seed. She came

first to a splendid mansion, knocked at the door, and said, "I am looking for a home that has never known sorrow. Is this such a place? It is very important to me." They told her, "You've certainly come to the wrong place," and began to describe all the tragic things that had recently befallen them.... She stayed to comfort them, then went on in her search for a home that had never known sorrow. But wherever she turned, in hovels and in palaces, she found one tale after another of sadness and misfortune.[9]

No human life stays free of pain. Ever since Adam's fall, we live in a broken world; we are, all of us, broken creatures.

Job: Indeed I know that this is so;
    but how can a mortal be just before God?
    ...He snatches away; who can stop him?
    Who will say to him, "What are you doing?"
    ...It is all one; therefore I say,
    he destroys both the blameless and the wicked.

    When disaster brings sudden death,
    he mocks at the calamity of the innocent.
    The earth is given into the hand of the wicked;
    he covers the eyes of its judges—
    if it is not he, who then is it?[10]

Julian: Let me tell you something that was shown to me—something so wondrous that I had to ponder it for twenty years before I understood it well enough to write it down. *I saw two persons..., a lord and a servant.... The lord sits in state, in rest and in peace. The servant stands before his lord, ready to do his lord's will. The lord looks on his servant*

*very lovingly and sweetly and mildly. He sends him to a
certain place to do his will. Not only does the servant go, but he
dashes off and runs at great speed.... And soon he falls into a
dell and is greatly injured; and then he groans and moans and
tosses about and writhes, but he cannot rise or help himself in
any way. And of all of this, the greatest hurt I saw him in was
lack of consolation, for he could not turn his face to look on his
loving lord.... [H]e paid heed to his feelings and his continuing
distress, in which distress he suffered seven great pains....*[11]

Job: I myself knew such pains. I could number them for
you: the pain of his injuries, his anger at his body, the
weakness he felt, his confusion and perplexity, his
inability to rise, his terrible aloneness, his great
discomfort and distress at the place in which he found
himself. Is that seven?

Julian: Rightly numbered! *And all this time his loving lord
looks on him most tenderly,...with great compassion and pity....*
*I saw ...that his great goodness and his own honour require
that his beloved servant, whom he loved so much, should be
highly and blessedly rewarded forever, above what he would
have been if he had not fallen, yes, and so much that his falling
and all the woe that he received from it will be turned into high,
surpassing honour and endless bliss....*
*I understood that the lord who sat in state in rest and peace
is God, I understood that the servant who stood before him was
shown for Adam, that is to say, one man was shown at that
time and his fall, so as to make it understood how God regards
all men and their falling. For in the sight of God all men are one
man, and one man is all men. This man was injured in his
powers and made most feeble.... And this is a great sorrow and
a cruel suffering to him, for he neither sees clearly his loving
lord, who is so meek and mild to him, nor does he truly see what
he himself is in the sight of his loving lord. And I know well*

that when these two things are wisely and truly seen, we shall
gain rest and peace, here in part and the fulness in the bliss of
heaven, by God's plentiful grace.[12]

Job: Nothing is harder than to see those two things: God
and ourselves through God's eyes. In my agony I
wondered if God had eyes as humans do. I prayed, both
to remind God and to reassure myself:

> Remember that you fashioned me like clay;
>   and will you turn me to dust again?
> Did you not pour me out like milk
>   and curdle me like cheese?
> You clothed me with skin and flesh,
>   and knit me together with bones and sinews.
> You have granted me life and steadfast love,
>   and your care has preserved my spirit.[13]

Julian: O my friends, Job's patience may be pious
imaginings, but his persistence in prayer is a model for all
of us! He seizes God as my cat seizes the thread trailing
from my needle: biting and pulling and tangling till he
gains my attention!

Not so his visiting friends. They spoke *about* God
while Job spoke *to* God; Job prayed. Prayer is most
needful to a broken race. Our courteous Lord welcomes
the praying soul, saying: *My dear darling, I am glad that you*
have come to me with all your woe. I have always been with
you, and now you see me loving, and we are made one in
bliss....

Our Lord is most glad and joyful because of our prayer, and
he expects it, and he wants to have it, for with his grace it
makes us like to himself...and such is his blessed will. For he
says: Pray wholeheartedly, though it seems to you that this has
no savour for you.... Pray wholeheartedly, though you may feel

nothing, though you may see nothing, yes, though you think
that you could not, for in dryness and in barrenness, in
sickness and in weakness, then is your prayer most pleasing to
me....[14]

And when we are most despondent, he will answer us
as he answered Saint Paul: "My grace is sufficient for
you, for power is made perfect in weakness."[15]

For the wonder is not that the little sparrow was
injured; the nature of cat and bird caused that. And it is
no wonder that the bird could never again soar to the
highest heavens, for neither my maidservant nor I
possessed the skills to mend such a marvel as a feathered
wing. The wonder is that it kept trying, that it did fly in
little fluttering hops and found joy in that small freedom.

Just so, the wonder is not that people suffer, for the
world holds pain and sorrow enough for all of us. Neither
need we wonder why God does not put things right
again, for God is already at work on the great deed; God
is already beginning to make all things well. No, the
wonder is that people who have been broken like
sparrows caught by a cat's claws should find three
strengths: the strength to go on living, the strength to
continue their search for God and the strength to reach
out to others, to give and receive compassion.

Job: Julian's wisdom puts me to shame. She is right:
People can withdraw into a shell when tragedy strikes,
pull their anguish around them like a blanket, refuse joy
and succumb to bitterness and despair. Have you ever
done that? I came close to it myself. I grieved that life had
been granted me:

> Why did I not die at birth,
>   come forth from the womb and expire?
> ...Or why was I not buried like a stillborn child,

like an infant that never sees the light?[16]

I have seen men in agony such as I knew throw
themselves upon their swords; I have seen women leap
from the rooftop. My life is empty of love and joy, yet
somehow I would rather be a bird whose wings beat
uselessly against the air than to seek the cat's merciful
bite.

Julian: The God who gave us life also gave us the
knowledge that life is precious. Why some people lose
that knowledge and put an end to their lives is beyond
my understanding; I cannot conceive such an act. Perhaps
some disease afflicts their reason. But it always makes me
wonder why people continue to say that God never gives
us more pain than we can bear. A woman repeated those
words at my window and asked me, "Then why did my
father kill himself?" I could only answer what I have said
before: God does not wish us pain; God holds us in love
most tender and wishes us naught save sweet merriment.

Some say it is death that makes life sweet, that because
our days are as fleeting as the daisy that sits in the jar on
my window sill, we count them as though they were
pearls.

That may or may not be true. I think not, for it says
here in my Bible that

...God did not make death,
and he does not delight in the death of the living.
For he created all things so that they might exist;
the generative forces of the world are wholesome,
and there is no destructive poison in them,
and the dominion of Hades is not on earth.
For righteousness is immortal.
But the ungodly by their words and deeds

81

summoned death....[17]

But certainly our vulnerability, the swift flight of our days and the fragility of our happiness, makes it necessary that we find love. From the moment we gasp our first breath, helpless in the midwife's hands, till we reach for a hand to hold as the darkness of death closes in on us, we crave human companionship. God shaped that need into new-forming clay.

Job: Loneliness was the worst of my pain. I complained that God

> ...has put my family far from me,
> > and my acquaintances are wholly estranged from
> > me.
> My relatives and my close friends have failed me;
> > the guests in my house have forgotten me;
> my serving girls count me as a stranger;
> > I have become an alien in their eyes.
> I call to my servant, but he gives me no answer;
> > I must myself plead with him.
> My breath is repulsive to my wife;
> > I am loathsome to my own family.
> Even young children despise me;
> > when I rise, they talk against me.
> All my intimate friends abhor me,
> > and those whom I loved have turned against me.[18]

Julian: Loneliness is the boon companion of suffering. All the people who sought consolation at my window said the same thing: "No one knows how I feel." Haven't you said the same, my friends? In truth, no one does. Each person's tragedy is a happening never seen on earth before, just as each person is an unrepeated and unrepeatable creation.

The young mother whose tiny daughter was seized by the bony arms of the Black Death wept, "I will never see her grow and bloom into womanhood." The woman whose daughter was embraced by the Death instead of by her promised bridegroom cried, "I watched her bloom only to see her die." The young man crippled by a toppling oxcart grieved for the loss of what he might have done; another, slowed by age, sorrowed that he could no longer do what he once did.

At the same time, suffering is universal. It follows each of us from the birthing bed to the grave. The infant in the midwife's hand draws in a breath of cold air and screams for the pain in its lungs. The dying release their last breath with a fearful groan.

Yet brokenness is not where our story ends. *For I saw most truly that always, as our contrariness makes for us here on earth pain, shame and sorrow, just so in contrary manner grace makes for us in heaven solace, honour and bliss, so superabundant that when we come up and receive that sweet reward which grace has made for us, there we shall thank and bless our Lord, endlessly rejoicing that we ever suffered woe; and that will be because of a property of the blessed love which we shall know in God, which we might never have known without woe preceding it.*[19]

Job: All humanity must then cry with me:

My face is red with weeping,
   and deep darkness is on my eyelids,
though there is no violence in my hands,
   and my prayer is pure....
My eye has grown dim from grief,
   and all my members are like a shadow....
My days are past, my plans are broken off,
   ...where then is my hope?

Will it go down to the bars of Sheol?
Shall we descend together into the dust?[20]

Julian: Ah, but suffering is not the whole story of our lives. Consider how our sweet Lord mothers us more tenderly than any human mother. *The mother may sometimes allow her child to fall and to be distressed in various ways, for its own benefit, but she can never suffer any kind of peril to come to her child, because of her love. And...our heavenly Mother Jesus may never suffer us who are his children to perish, for he is almighty, all wisdom and all love, and so is none but he, blessed may he be....*

And then he wants us to show a child's characteristics, which always naturally trusts in its mother's love in well-being and in woe. And he wants us to commit ourselves fervently to the faith of Holy Church, and find there our beloved Mother in consolation and true understanding, with all the company of the blessed. For one single person may be broken, as it seems to him, but the entire body of Holy Church was never broken, nor ever will be without end....

And he revealed this in these gracious words: I protect you very safely.[21]

In the Church our loneliness is dispelled, for there God's loving arms gather together all of us in all our brokenness.

Listen: Do you hear the bells? They are calling God's people to Vespers. It is time to reflect on the things we have talked about, time to say our evening psalm and settle ourselves under God's wings for the night. May sweet dreams of God's love remain with you until dawn.

For Reflection

- *The sparrow's injury resulted from the nature of Julian's cat.* To what extent can you trace your sorrow to the nature of the world, to the brokenness of the human condition?

- *In what ways is your suffering different from anyone else's? In what ways is it like another's?*

- *How do you, like Saint Paul, struggle with human brokenness? Are you able, like Job, to persist in prayer?*

- *What keeps you going?*

- *What consolation have you found in the Church?*

Closing Prayer

(Group response: "Lord, hear my voice!")

Out of the depths I cry to you, O Lord.
   Lord, hear my voice!
Let your ears be attentive
   to the voice of my supplications!

If you, O Lord, should mark iniquities,
   Lord, who could stand?
But there is forgiveness with you,
   so that you may be revered.

I wait for the Lord, my soul waits,
   and in his word I hope;
my soul waits for the Lord
   more than those who watch for the morning,
   more than those who watch for the morning.

O Israel, hope in the Lord!
   For with the Lord there is steadfast love,
   and with him is great power to redeem.
It is he who will redeem Israel

from all its iniquities.[22]

Notes

[1] *A Treasury of Jewish Folklore: Stories, Traditions, Legends, Humor, Wisdom and Folk Songs of the Jewish People*, edited by Nathan Ausubel, abridged by Alan Mintz (New York: Bantam Books, 1980), pp. 327-328.

[2] Job 29:1-6.

[3] *Showings*, p. 321.

[4] Job 14:1-2, 7-10.

[5] *Showings*, pp. 320-321.

[6] *Showings*, p. 321.

[7] *Showings*, p. 259.

[8] Romans 7:15, 19-20, 22-24.

[9] *When Bad Things Happen to Good People*, by Harold S. Kushner (New York: Schocken Books, 1981), pp. 110-111.

[10] Job 9:2, 12, 22-24.

[11] *Showings*, p. 267.

[12] *Showings*, pp. 268-271.

[13] Job 10:8-12.

[14] *Showings*, pp. 246, 249.

[15] 2 Corinthians 12:9.

[16] Job 3:11, 16.

[17] Wisdom 1:13-16a.

[18] Job 19:13-19.

[19] *Showings*, p. 263.

[20] Job 16:16-17; 17:7, 11a, 15-16.

[21] *Showings*, pp. 300-302.

[22] Psalm 130.

DAY FIVE
Seeking Support

Coming Together in the Spirit

In the 1977 film *Oh, God!* an unlikely deity played by George Burns intrudes into the life of Jerry Landers, a supermarket manager played by John Denver. He has come, God explains, to send Landers to the world with a message—to be another Moses. Landers protests that he is not a believer; he hasn't much use for religion and is not in the habit of going to church.

"Religion is easy," God retorts. "I'm talking about faith.... Even nonbelievers want what they've got down here to work. That's why I came: to tell everybody I set the world up so it can work. Only it's up to you. You can't look to me to do it for you.... I don't get into details. I gave you a world and everything in it. It's all up to you."

Landers continues to argue. "If you're so involved with us, how can you permit all the suffering that goes on in the world?"

God is indignant. "How can *I* permit the suffering? I don't permit the suffering; you do. All the choices are yours. You can love each other; you can nurture each other; you can kill each other. I gave you a world and everything in it. It's all up to you."

"But we need help," stammers Landers.

God smiles. "That's why I gave you each other."

Defining Our Thematic Context

Suffering people's search for understanding is more than a search for reasons. Reasons ultimately fail to ease pain; human wisdom cannot account for it satisfactorily. The agonized *why* on Job's lips or yours is less a plea for an explanation than a cry for understanding and comfort.

Job's friends came to comfort him but, when they lapsed into explaining his plight, they not only failed in their attempt but also added to his misery. Julian was a much wiser counselor. So tenderly did she minister to the wounded souls who approached her window that Norwich townsfolk called the anchoress at St. Julian's Church "Mother Julian."

Bring your need for comfort, your desire to give comfort to others, to your mentors. In this session they will explore with you the power—and the failures—of the believing community.

Opening Prayer

Job, weary sufferer,
you sought consolation
and found condemnation;
you sought understanding,
and your friends offered only reasons.
Lend me your persistence in truth,
your strength to refute false comforters.
Support me with your faith
that God cares for the wounded,
that comfort can and should be found
in the community of believers.

Julian, mother and consoler,
Hear my cries for understanding.

Lend me your listening ear,
your listening heart.
Comfort my troubled soul.
Help me to believe that
in the company of believers
I will find the assurance
that all will indeed be well;
every manner of thing will be well.

Wise mentors,
guide me in my search for consolation,
in my search for companionship
in this darkness that overwhelms me.

RETREAT SESSION FIVE

Job: I saw them coming, distant figures on camelback
shimmering against the sun-burned sand. When they
drew near enough that I could make out their faces, my
heart leaped with joy. "It's Eliphaz the Temanite!" I cried.
"With him is Bildad the Shuite, and the third—surely it's
Zophar the Naamathite! Good friends they have always
been to me. Surely here is balm for my aching heart."

And balm they were. They tore their garments and
heaped the desert dust on their heads in mourning. They
sat beside me, rocking in silent commiseration for seven
days and seven nights, and their nearness was sweet
consolation.

But when I gave voice to my misery, Eliphaz turned
on me.

Think now, who that was innocent ever perished?
  Or where were the upright cut off?
As I have seen, those who plow iniquity
  and sow trouble reap the same.
By the breath of God they perish,
  and by the blast of his anger they are consumed....
How happy is the one whom God reproves;
  therefore do not despise the discipline of the
    Almighty.[1]

I tried to answer him, to justify my complaint and expose
the breadth of my suffering. But scarce had my words left
my mouth when Bildad had his say.

Does God pervert justice?
  Or does the Almighty pervert the right?
If your children sinned against him,
  he delivered them into the power of their
    transgression.
If you will seek God
  and make supplication to the Almighty,
if you are pure and upright,
  surely then he will rouse himself for you
  and restore to you your rightful place.[2]

How dare he impute blame for my tribulations upon my
children! How can I contend with God? I asked him. I
cannot evade the traps God sets for me.
  Then Zophar dealt the cruelest blow of all, turning on
me in bitter betrayal.

Should your babble put others to silence,
  and when you mock, shall no one shame you?
For you say, "My conduct is pure,
  and I am clean in God's sight.
But oh, that God would speak
  and open his lips to you...

> Know then that God exacts of you less than your
> guilt deserves.[3]

Let God speak, indeed! As I told the three of them:

> What you know, I also know;
>   I am not inferior to you.
> But I would speak to the Almighty,
>   and I desire to argue my case with God.
> As for you, you whitewash with lies;
>   all of you are worthless physicians.
> If you would only keep silent,
>   that would be your wisdom![4]

Were those three not thorn enough, another came along
later—a young whippersnapper who thought he could
make a better case. But Elihu only repeated what my
friends had said and attacked me for crying out:

> Those who have sense will say to me,
>   and the wise who hear me will say,
> "Job speaks without knowledge,
>   his words are without insight.
> Would that Job were tried to the limit,
>   because his answers are those of the wicked.
> For he adds rebellion to his sin;
>   he claps his hands among us,
>   and multiplies his words against God."[5]

Julian: Be not too harsh with them, Job. Remember how
sweet it was when the three sat with you in silence. Know
that all through those seven days they sought words with
which to comfort you—words that would also ease their
discomfort in the face of your agony. They searched their
souls and gave you the best they had, the only wisdom
they had learned. They had not, like you, been schooled

in suffering; they had not yet felt its scourge. They knew not how tender scars on the soul can be. Have you not known such useless physicians, my friends?

Because suffering has not yet touched them, they can be at peace with platitudes. As we discussed earlier, only those who have worked their way through sorrow can find the bit of truth in the answers human wisdom raises to woe. When they come from the mouths of those who have not yet known pain, suffering exposes religious platitudes for what they are—false comfort—and sets the sufferer off in search of deeper understanding of God's ways.

Do you know the story of Jacob? God seized him one night and they wrestled until daybreak. The struggle left Jacob with a limp that never healed, but it also gained him his identity. From that night on, the name he bore was Israel. It was a name not only for a man, but for a people who together walked with God.[6]

Job: But how can a people who, as you say, together walk with God so often misspeak God's ways so badly?

Julian: Because we are merely mortals and cannot grasp the whole reality of God. We acknowledge God's power and wisdom without resting in God's love and goodwill toward us, *for some of us believe that God is almighty and may do everything, and that he is all wisdom and can do everything, but that he is all love and wishes to do everything, there we fail. And it is this ignorance which most hinders God's lovers, as I see it…. For of all the attributes of the blessed Trinity, it is God's will that we have most faithfulness and delight in love.*[7]

And so in every age there are some who cling to religious platitudes. The people who offer them as easy answers believe—rightly—that the Lord will make all things well, and that he can. What they overlook is the depth of God's tenderness, how sweetly the Lord yearns to make all things well, how merry and glad it will make him.

And their experience is too narrow to take into account what agony their brothers and sisters face. Because they cannot conceive the depth of others' pain, neither can they conceive the depth of the Lord's tender pity for those who suffer. They have not grasped the height and breadth and depth of God's love and compassion. The four who added to your torment were such as these, as are the people who have offered only hollow comfort to you, my friends.

Job: Then I was right to insist that only God could answer my appeal. There is no comfort to be found among believers.

Julian: Not so! Listen: Do you know this prayer?

God our Father,
we had wandered far from you,
but through your Son you have brought us back.
You gave him up to death
so that we might turn again to you
and find our way to one another.[8]

Holy Church is not only the place where we seek to know more of God; it is also the place where we find one another. Your pastors, my friends, have described us as a pilgrim people who belong to this age, who carry the mark of a world which will pass, who with all creatures groan and travail while we await the fulfillment of God's ends.[9]

It is fitting that we should support one another on our

journey, that we should share whatever insights into God's ways we have been given. That is why I made my showings known.

Everything I say about me I mean to apply to all my fellow Christians, for I am taught that this is what our Lord intends in this spiritual revelation.... God, ...out of his courteous love and his endless goodness was willing to show it generally, to the comfort of us all....

If I pay special attention to myself, I am nothing at all; but in general I am, I hope, in the unity of love with all my fellow Christians.... For God is everything that is good, as I see; and God has made everything that is made, and God loves everything that he has made. And he who has general love for all his fellow Christians in God has love towards everything that is.

But in everything I believe as Holy Church preaches and teaches. For the faith of the Holy Church was always in my sight.... And to this end I contemplated the revelation with all diligence....

All this was shown in three parts, that is to say, by bodily vision and by words formed in my understanding and by spiritual vision. But I may not and cannot show the spiritual visions as plainly and as fully as I should. But I trust in our Lord God almighty that he will, out of his goodness and for love of you, make you accept it more spiritually and more sweetly than I can or may tell it.[10]

Job: But when the only comfort religious people can speak is hollow words, what profit is there in Church?

Julian: Job's friends had a point: He does not listen well, does he? Four misspeaking men are not the Church! A band of pilgrims must slow their pace to that of the slowest in the party. And the slowest are not just those who have been wounded on the journey. The little ones, the tiny children clinging to their mothers' skirts, also slow the trek. Think of those who have not yet learned to speak of God's ways with us as little children, still innocent of suffering, still ignorant of God's great love for us. The band with whom we travel is a vast throng, spread across the face of the earth and the vast reaches of history. One believer may speak foolishly; so may ten or a hundred. Even those who preach cannot be expected to be perfectly wise, for Holy Church is an imperfect people on a journey toward Truth.

We span centuries. Living and dead, all who seek God with sincere hearts have been joined by God in a great communion. How else could Job and I be here with you today? For *all the help that we have from particular saints and from all the blessed company of heaven, the precious love and the holy, endless friendship that we have from them, it is of his goodness. For the intermediaries which the goodness of God has ordained to help us are very lovely and many.*[11]

And words are secondary to us; our first language is ritual. As surely as the Church introduces us to faith, it gives us ritual to assure us that no one need face life's crises alone—neither moments of great travail nor moments of joy so great it can break a heart.

Louder than our voices speak the signs we make as our Lord commanded. From the window in my cell I watched the bread being broken, the wine poured out like spilled blood. And I saw my Lord as he showed himself to me: *I saw the red blood running down from under the crown, hot and flowing freely and copiously, a living stream, just as it was at the time the crown of thorns was pressed on his blessed head.*[12]

Then it came to my mind that God has created bountiful waters on the earth for our use and our bodily comfort, out of the tender love he has for us. But it is more pleasing to him that we accept for our total cure his blessed blood to wash us of our sins, for there is no drink that is made which pleases him so well to give us.[13]

Do you remember when, a few years ago, the earth trembled beneath Mexico City and brought great buildings crashing down upon the inhabitants? A woman lay buried under the rubble for many days, clutching her infant to her heart. She kept the child alive long past the time rescue workers hoped to find survivors by letting it suck the blood from her wounds. So does Christ our Mother nourish us.

Job: Christ our Mother? You have called him that before. But was not Christ a man?

Julian: Yes, but nonetheless he is surely our true mother. *We know that our mothers bear us for pain and death. O, what is that? But our true Mother Jesus, he alone bears us for joy and for endless life, blessed may he be. So he carries us within him in love and travail, until the full time when he wanted to suffer the sharpest thorns and cruel pains that ever were or will be, and at the last he died. And when he had finished, and had borne us so for bliss, still all this could not satisfy his wonderful love....*

The mother can give her child to suck of her milk, but our precious Mother Jesus can feed us with himself, and does, most courteously and tenderly....[14]

We were talking about ritual, something in which a mother quickly becomes an expert, for she sees her child take comfort from it. She tucks her babe into the cradle with the same lullaby night after night, and the infant, hearing her voice, knows it is safe to slip into the little death of sleep. She rubs the little one's body with oil after a bath, and the sweet smell erases the infant's fear of the water. She plays peek-a-boo, reassuring her little one that she will come back even if she leaves for a while.

And when the dog barks or the thunder roars, she rocks her child, patting the babe's back and murmuring, "It's all right; everything's all right." Mind you, she knows full well that the dog's teeth are sharp, that the wind may lift the thatch from the roof, that lightning has fearsome power—even that her babe does not understand her words.

So it is with the rituals of religion. We anoint our sick with sweet-smelling oils and waft incense that rises to God like a released soul over our dead. We welcome a child born anew in the font into our family and rub in the confirming oil. With joy we receive back into our company those who have turned away from us for a while, celebrate the union of man and woman in marriage and the commitment of men and women to lives of service to Holy Church. Above all, we share the family meal our Mother Jesus has prepared for us.

Job: I have performed rituals myself. I used to rise early in the morning and offer burnt offerings in case any of my household had displeased God. The fragrant smoke carried my prayer toward God.

Julian: Our prayer, too, rises to God. But it also strikes our own ears. We tell of all God has done for us:

> You formed us in your own likeness
> and set us over the world
> to serve you, our creator,
> and to rule over all creatures....
> Again and again you offered a covenant to us,
> and through the prophets taught us to hope for
>   salvation.
> Father, you so loved the world
> that in the fullness of time you sent your only Son to

be our Savior....

> To the poor he proclaimed the good news of
>   salvation,
> to prisoners, freedom,
> and to those in sorrow, joy.[15]

Even in my day, when Mass was in Latin and we common folk did not understand the language which framed our prayer, we knew their sense. How fortunate are you, my friends! Your public worship is cast in your own tongue; you can hear the words and know their meaning.

At Mass, we remind God of what he has done before and ask that he have pity on us again, yes. But we also tell one another in God's overhearing what God has done in order to bolster our own hopes, to strengthen our own faith that he will welcome us to heaven.

Job: Heaven—that's an idea that arose after my time. And I have heard it used to justify much suffering in this life. "Be patient with your lot; bear your burdens without complaint, and you will know great joy in heaven": That is what the rich tell the poor, what the powerful say to the oppressed. Heaven seems very distant to those who suffer *now*, does it not, friends?

Julian: Ah, but the promise is precious! A woman endures great anguish to bring a child to birth. Yet when the midwife lays the babe in her arms, she counts the travail of little import, so great is her joy. Thus so, the Lord said to me: *Suddenly you will be taken out of all your pain, all your sickness, all your unrest and all your woe. And you will come up above, and you will have me for your reward, and you will be filled full of joy and bliss, and you will never again have any kind of pain, any kind of sickness, any kind of* *displeasure, no lack of will, but always joy and bliss without end. Why then should it afflict you to endure awhile, since it is my will and to my glory?*[16]

Still, it is a grave sin to use the promises of faith as an excuse for inaction. Because God plans such consolation for us, God's people are bound to do what lies in their power to ease one another's sorrow.

Eliphaz, Bildad and Zophar knew that well; the knowledge brought them to the land of Uz to comfort Job. Their fault, if fault it can be called, was that no person, no happening had taught them *how* to give comfort.

Those who have walked the valley of darkness know better how to strengthen another's steps. They know what comforts and what does not.

Job: Truly spoken. When I opened my hands to the orphan, the widow, the poor, I knew not their hearts' need. I gave freely of my goods; I fed their bodies but not their souls. Knew I then what I know now, I would have asked them to sit with me and tell their stories. And I would have listened, and held their hands and wept with them. It is the schooling in sorrow I have known that brings me here to pray with you today, friends. I have not Julian's mothering skills, but I have gained an empathetic ear.

Julian: Just so. A woman whose own child lay in the grave tells of visiting casual acquaintances after their son's death:

> They had a house full of people. Yet when they saw us they left everyone and asked us to sit with them in another room. The father put his head on my husband's shoulder and cried. My husband held the

newly bereaved man in his arms and patted him and quieted him. The mother grasped my hands and cried.

We did not possess some secret knowledge that gave us special comforting skills. What we had was something few could give them. We had experience. When they saw us, they saw a mother and father with a dead child who were able to cope.[17]

The good people of Norwich made pilgrimage to my cell window because they knew I would not offer them platitudes. They knew I had been in the dark valley of sickness and loss; they knew that I had come back from that dread place with a listening heart.

Just so, we come to the Lord Jesus because he bears the wounds of human suffering in his body. In his company and in the company of his people we will find, if we seek, listening hearts. In his company and in the company of his people we will also find compassion and healing.

And so let us seek together. Take a moment to consider the ways in which people can truly comfort one another, and then let us begin our evening prayer. The ancient psalmist has given us words to frame our need. Let us trust that the great throng which has prayed them for uncounted generations will join their voices to ours in the hymn of praise that will never end.

For Reflection

- *Has anyone tried to comfort you with religious platitudes? How did you react?*

- *Have you ever tried to distance yourself from another's pain with religious platitudes? What would you do differently now?*

- To whom have you gone for comfort? What led you to that person?

- From whom have you gained comfort? How?

- How real is the Communion of Saints to you? To what saints—canonized saints or holy people you have known or know of—do you pray? Why?

Closing Prayer

(Group response: "Praise God in the company of the upright.")

Praise the LORD!
I will give thanks to the LORD with my whole heart,
  in the company of the upright, in the
    congregation.
Great are the works of the LORD,
  studied by all who delight in them.
Full of honor and majesty is his work,
  and his righteousness endures forever.

He has gained renown by his wonderful deeds;
  the LORD is gracious and merciful.
He provides food for those who fear him;
  he is ever mindful of his covenant.
He has shown his people the power of his works,
  in giving them the heritage of the nations.

The works of his hands are faithful and just;
  all his precepts are trustworthy.
They are established forever and ever,
  to be performed with faithfulness and
    uprightness.
He sent redemption to his people;

he has commanded his covenant forever.
Holy and awesome is his name.
The fear of the LORD is the beginning of wisdom;
all those who practice it have a good
understanding.
His praise endures forever.[18]

Notes

[1] Job 4:7-9; 5:17.

[2] Job 8:3-6.

[3] Job 11:3-5a, 6b.

[4] Job 13:2-5.

[5] Job 34:34-37.

[6] See Genesis 32:22-32.

[7] *Showings*, p. 323.

[8] Eucharistic Prayer for Masses of Reconciliation II, translation by International Commission for English in the Liturgy, Inc., Washington, D.C. (1975).

[9] *Constitution on the Church*, #48.

[10] *Showings*, pp. 191-192.

[11] *Showings*, p. 185.

[12] *Showings*, p. 181.

[13] *Showings*, p. 200.

[14] *Showings*, pp. 297-298.

[15] Eucharistic Prayer IV, translation by International Commission for English in the Liturgy, Inc., Washington, D.C. (1969).

[16] *Showings*, p. 306.

[17] *The Bereaved Parent*, by Harriet Sarnoff Schiff (New York: Crown Publishers, Inc., 1977), p. xii.

[18] Psalm 111.

Day Six

Learning Compassion

Coming Together in the Spirit

All slaves are called Bark, so Bark was his name. But despite four years of captivity he could not resign himself to it and remembered constantly that he had been a king.... "I was a drover, and my name was Mohammed!"

[His] freedom had come too suddenly: Bark was finding it hard to orient himself.... He idled in front of the Jewish shops, stared at the sea, repeated to himself that he could walk as he pleased in any direction, that he was free. But this freedom had in it a taste of bitterness: what he learned from it with most intensity was that he had no ties with the world....

But when, rounding a corner, he came upon a group of children at play, he stopped. This was it. He stared at them in silence. Then he went off to the Jewish shops and came back laden with treasure....

Solemnly he beckoned to each child in turn, and the little hands rose towards the toys and the bangles and the gold-sewn slippers.... Other children in Agadir, hearing the news, ran after him; and these too were shod by Bark in golden slippers. The tale spread to the outskirts of town, whence still other children scurried into town....

[A]mong these children, he felt the pull of his

true weight. Like an archangel who had cheated,
had sewn lead into his girdle, Bark dragged himself
forward, pulling against the pull of a thousand
children who had such great need of golden
slippers.[1]

Defining Our Thematic Context

An emancipated slave's reckless generosity to a horde
of barefoot street urchins brings to believers' minds
another who, in Saint Paul's words,

...though he was in the form of God,
    did not regard equality with God
    as something to be exploited,
but emptied himself,
    taking the form of a slave,
    being born in human likeness.[2]

It was Jesus Christ, crucified slave and risen Lord, whose
great compassion gave barefoot prisoners in the cotton
fields and slave cabins of the American South the hope to
sing, "O dem golden slippers!"

The wounded people who gather in his name ever
place their trust in his compassion. Together they dog his
steps, straggling along his way like refugees from a war
zone, one supporting another, the strong carrying the
weak, pausing to bind up one another's wounds or to dry
a tear-stained cheek.

For compassion toward others is not just a nice
Christian option, but an essential part of following the
Lord who identified himself with the hungry and the
naked, the sick and the imprisoned.[3] As the great
humanitarian Albert Schweitzer put it, "Those who bear
the mark of pain are never really free, for they owe a debt

to the ones who still suffer."
Job cried out for compassion; Julian dispensed it freely
from her cell. Today they invite you to take heart from
their wisdom.

Opening Prayer

Job, complaining friend,
you based your claim to innocence before God
in the compassion you showed
to widow and orphan,
to servant and stranger.
Lend me your generous heart,
teach me to open mine.
Support me with your firm belief
that God is with the caring,
that God's friendship ever belongs
to those who extend the divine gift of compassion.

Julian, mild anchoress,
share with me your Lord's compassion.
Teach me the art of condolence,
how to touch the lives of others
with the healing you dispensed from your cell.
Help me to find the strength
that grows out of weakness,
The wholeness that only the broken can gain.

Help me to believe
and to pass on to others
the certainty that all will indeed be well;
every manner of thing will be well.

RETREAT SESSION SIX

Julian: The other day I told you only part of the showing that baffled my understanding for so many years. I spoke of a great lord who sat in state, and of the servant sent on an errand who fell into a dell and was grievously injured. The lord I took to be God, and the servant, Adam.

But there was more to the showing. Again *I saw the lord sitting in state, and the servant standing respectfully before his lord...; his clothing was a white tunic, scanty, old and all worn, dyed with the sweat of his body, tight fitting and short, ...looking threadbare as if it would soon be worn out, ready to go to rags and to tear. And in this I was much amazed, thinking: This is not fitting clothing for a servant so greatly loved to stand in before so honourable a lord.... And by the inward perception which I had of both the lord and the servant, it seemed that he was newly appointed, that is to say just beginning to serve, and that this servant had never been sent out before....*

Finally I came to understand that the servant is both the sweet Christ and Adam, and that Adam represents all of us, for we all fell with him. And when Adam fell, God's Son chose to fall with him because of the great love which has bound God to Adam's race from the very beginning.

God's Son fell with Adam, into the valley of the womb of the maiden who was the fairest daughter of Adam...for the divinity rushed from the Father into the maiden's womb, falling to accept our nature, and in this falling he took great hurt.... By his tunic being ready to go to rags is understood the rods and the scourges, the thorns and the nails, the pulling and the dragging and the tearing of his tender flesh.... [H]e could never with almighty power rise from the time he fell into the maiden's womb until his body was slain and dead, and he had yielded his soul into the Father's hand, with all mankind for whom he had been sent....

The body lay in the grave until Easter morning, and from that time it never lay again.... Adam's old tunic, tight-fitting, threadbare and short, was then made lovely by our saviour, new, white and bright and forever clean....[4]

Job: Over the centuries I have heard many tales of gods walking in human guise for a while. Even the God of Israel, they say, strolled with Adam in the garden in the cool of the evening and came down for a bargaining session with Abraham over the fate of Sodom and Gomorrah.[5] But only in the story of Jesus have I heard that God became truly human, truly one with us in all our pain and sorrow.

Julian: Truly one of us he is—"like us in all things but sin"[6]—so that we may be like him.

Job: Like God? I thought that was Adam's sin—wanting to be like God.

Julian: Adam wanted to *be* God, not to be, as God had planned, *one with* God. Christ has set Adam's wrong right and brought us into the blessed oneness that was God's wise design from the beginning.

I often wondered why, through the great prescient wisdom of God, the beginning of sin was not prevented. For then it seemed to me that all would have been well....

But Jesus...answered with these words and said: Sin is necessary.... [7] Have you not heard the song Christians raise on the Vigil of Easter to celebrate his Resurrection?

Father, how wonderful your care for us!
How boundless your merciful love!

To ransom a slave
you gave away your Son.

O happy fault, O necessary sin of Adam,
which gained for us so great a Redeemer![8]

Job: What strange thinking! Now I understand why the thought of the Deuteronomist—that God must reward the good and punish the wicked—endures so strongly. It makes more sense.

Julian: It makes sense, yes—but only in human terms. How our race does love logic! But Saint Paul assured us that a greater power than reason rules the universe:

For Jews demand signs and Greeks desire wisdom, but we proclaim Christ crucified, a stumbling block to Jews and foolishness to Gentiles, but to those who are the called, both Jews and Greeks, Christ the power of God and the wisdom of God. For God's foolishness is wiser than human wisdom, and God's weakness is stronger than human strength.[9]

In Christ God showed the strength that can grow from our brokenness, the ability our pain gives us, if we let it, to empathize with another's pain and become, like God, full of compassion. *So I saw how Christ has compassion on us...; and just as I was before filled full of pain on account of Christ's Passion, so I was now in a measure filled with compassion for all my fellow Christians, and then I saw that every kind of compassion which one has for one's fellow Christians in love is Christ in us.*[10]

Job: There is truth in what you say. I know a man who lived in your own century, friends—not a Christian, but a Jew given the name Mietek at his circumcision. I feel a bond with him because our stories are so similar. Like me, he lost everything he loved—his family, his home. And he lost it all not once, but twice.

Mietek was fourteen when Nazi hordes overran his native Warsaw. The Jews were sealed into the ghetto, and for a while war was just a game a boy might play—a dangerous game, but a game nonetheless. He matched wits with the conquerors, slipping in and out of the ghetto for food. But then the Nazis drove the Jews into a new and terrible exile in Treblinka.

There the lives of Mietek's mother and younger brothers were snuffed out by a deadly cloud. Martin, young and strong, went to the labor force. Hunger roared in his belly; a blow from a guard's weapon struck out one eye. He was cast into the depths of Sheol, into the bowels of Treblinka, and forced to carry the bodies of his people from the gas chamber to mass graves dug in the yellow sand.

Amazingly, he escaped. He journeyed back to Warsaw just in time to take part in the doomed ghetto uprising. He watched his own father, the last surviving member of his family, crumple to the street in a hail of Nazi bullets.

Again he fled the spreading horror. Mietek skulked in the forest with other warriors to ambush and kill Germans. One day he and his comrades spread a net for an SS troop.

> We didn't leave a German alive. Only their black bodies reddened the snow. I stared at each one of them in turn; I prized their stiffening fingers from their weapons. Bolek came up to me.
> "We've avenged them, Mietek."
> I shook my head. We'd never been avenged. The deaths of butchers didn't restore life; revenge was always bitter.

"Even if we kill them all, Bolek, my brothers won't come back to life again.... We're killing too, Bolek. We're killing."[11]

As he fought the beast without, Mietek feared the beast within. Marching into defeated Berlin with the Russian army, he watched the soldiers lay rough hands on German civilians. To a companion he said:

"We've got to be careful, Jurek, now we're the stronger. We've got to be men twice over."
All night I lay awake: I could see the civilians, their faces covered with welts from the soldiers' blows. They had the look of men who didn't understand what was happening to them, victims of their obedience. Mietek, Mietek, be careful! It's easy to become a butcher.[12]

When the enemy was at last defeated, Mietek built a new life as Martin Gray, a trader in antiques. He took to wife a beautiful woman. Together they restored a crumbling chateau in the south of France, where they welcomed four precious children.

One night the woods went ablaze; flames roared all around them. Dina and the children fled toward safety in their car, while Martin followed on his motorcycle. Martin reached safety, but his wife and little ones were trapped by a surge of flame. They perished.

Does Martin Gray's story not remind you of mine? *The LORD said to Satan, "Very well, he is in your power; only spare his life."*[13] Martin Gray spent his season wailing on the trash dump, a man seemingly cursed by God. But he then channeled his grief into making the world safe for other families through the Dina Gray Foundation, dedicated to the protection of human life.

Julian: Martin's story calls to my mind what the Lord Jesus showed to me: *And these words, You will not be overcome, were said very insistently and strongly, for certainty and strength against every tribulation which may come. He did not say: You will not be assailed, you will not be belaboured, you will not be disquieted, but he said: You will not be overcome. God wants us to pay attention to his words, and always to be strong in our certainty, in well-being and in woe, for he loves us and delights in us, and so he wishes us to love him and delight in him and trust greatly in him, and all will be well.*[14]

I have seen many people, grievously wounded, face life with courage and compassion. They limp, they fly in fluttering hops on a badly mended wing, but they bring hope and comfort to a world no less wounded than they.

Some have found a place in history for the great things they accomplished. A woman from my own dear island, Cicely Saunders, watched her husband die a lonely death of cancer, his suffering prolonged by the skills of medical art. A physician herself, the grieving widow founded the hospice movement. Thanks to her compassion, people can leave this world as they did in my day, kept comfortable by the healing arts, surrounded by their loved ones, surrendering their lives to God in peace.

In another age, a black slave named Harriet Tubman fled Maryland and made her way to freedom in the northern United States. Seeing in the eye of her understanding the oppression her people suffered, she journeyed back to the South many times, putting herself in great peril. She guided more than three hundred of her brothers and sisters through swamps and woods, eluding the slave catchers and their dogs. Moses, they called her, for she led her people to freedom.

There are many more: Comedian Danny Thomas built

on the memory of failure and near-despair a hospital for desperately ill children, St. Jude's, the City of Hope. Father Maximilian Kolbe traded his life for the life of a man with a wife and children in a Nazi prison camp. Holy Church calls him a saint, a martyr for charity.

When Candy Lightner's daughter was struck and killed by a drunken driver, her grief and rage gave birth to a movement dedicated to enforcing laws against such deadly abuse of alcohol: Mothers Against Drunk Driving (MADD).

A man descended from slaves, Martin Luther King, Jr., inspired a generation with his eloquence and courage. A minister of the gospel, he preached to believers of all races the blessed truth Saint Paul prayed they might know:

> I pray that you may have the power to comprehend, with all the saints, what is the breadth and length and height and depth, and to know the love of Christ that surpasses knowledge, so that you may be filled with all the fullness of God. Now to him who by the power at work within us is able to accomplish abundantly far more than all we can ask or imagine, to him be glory in the church and in Christ Jesus to all generations, forever and ever. Amen.[15]

Job: It is not just those whom history remembers who accomplish great things. Many more do small deeds and never know the power they wield. When my friends sat *shiva* with me those first days after their coming, their silent presence was a greater comfort than I can speak. Sometimes an understanding smile or a gentle touch is sweeter than a juicy pomegranate.

Julian: Our gracious Lord most courteously promised the

Kingdom to those who offer only small gifts. A cup of water for a thirsty throat, an hour's company for the sick and imprisoned, a shoulder wet with another's tears— such things he stores in his royal treasury.[16] *And at the end of woe, suddenly our eyes will be opened, and in the clearness of our sight our light will be full.... This light is charity, ...such a light as we can live in meritoriously, with labour deserving the honourable thanks of God.... So charity keeps us in faith and in hope. And faith and hope lead us in charity, and in the end everything will be charity.*[17]

The Lord values such gifts even more than what we ordinarily call righteousness. The Holocaust of this century was surely as great an evil as the world has ever seen. It brought suffering on an undreamed-of scale into the world. Yet in every land it blighted, some people resisted its horror with compassion. Among them was a man whom no one would have judged righteous. Oskar Schindler was a man driven by ruthless greed, a notorious womanizer and accomplished briber. He saw an opportunity to build a fortune on the labor of Jewish slaves and courted the Nazis who could provide it.

Then one day the sight of a child headed for certain extermination, a weeping little girl in a bright red coat, called forth in his heart a depth of compassion no one—least of all Schindler—had ever known existed. Nazi eyes saw no change in him. The twelve hundred Jews he saved from the gas chambers knew better. To them he was a holy man, a blessed savior to whom they could bring their relatives and friends. He put his reputation for venality to God's purposes.

Job: Schindler was not himself a survivor of persecution. Whence came this compassion?

Julian: It could only have come from the grace and mercy with which God surrounds us all. Job's friends had it wrong, didn't they, my friends? God showers us with divine favor before we do anything to earn it. My Bible says, "God proves his love for us in that while we still were sinners Christ died for us."[18]

God's mercy shows motherly care, for a mother's love is tender and compassionate. God's generously given grace reveals the nature of his kingship, for only in the royal dominion of God's love can such a store of wealth exist. God's mercy and grace are constantly at work in our world.

Mercy works, protecting, enduring, vivifying and healing, and it is all of the tenderness of love; and grace works with mercy, raising, rewarding, endlessly exceeding what our love and labour deserve, distributing and displaying the vast plenty and generosity of God's royal dominion in his wonderful courtesy. And this is from the abundance of love, for grace transforms our dreadful failing into plentiful and endless solace; and grace transforms our shameful falling into high and honourable rising....[19]

And the more we come to know the depth of our Mother's mercy and the breadth of our great King's grace, *the more...shall we long to be filled with endless joy and bliss, for we are made for this. And our natural substance is now full of blessedness in God, and has been since it was made, and will be without end.*[20]

My friends, every human community is blessed by our loving God with someone who has the ability to leap the bounds of personal experience and enter into the suffering of another. They seldom know how graced they are, what grace they are. But others do. Look at Job: Before he ever shed a tear, he was a man to whom people with hearts full of tears came.

Job: What else could I do?

Surely one does not turn against the needy,
when in disaster they cry for help.
Did I not weep for those whose day was hard?
Was not my soul grieved for the poor?....
Did not he who made me in the womb make them?
And did not one fashion us in the womb?[21]

But if there was in my village a gentle Mother Julian,
word of her did not reach my ear as I sat on the dump.
The people of Norwich were wiser than I: They sought
her out. Follow their lead, friends; search for
understanding hearts.

Julian: They sought me out thinking that, because I spent
my day in solitary prayer, I had some special divine
gift—perhaps even the power to work a miracle. But the
only power vouchsafed to me was a showing of Christ
crucified, in which I saw his sweet compassion.

I did what my Bible told me Jesus did. I asked the
question he asked the blind man: "What do you want me
to do for you?" Had they thought me the Christ, they
would no doubt have answered as that man did: "Let me
see again."[22] Knowing my limits, they asked me to do
only what did lie within my power: to listen, to weep
with them and pray for them, to help them seek a way
through the darkness.

It is not compassion that is lacking in our world, but
knowledge of how to express it. We like not to see a
dumb animal suffer, much less one of our own kind.

When my cat came back from courting with an ear
torn by another tom, I hastened to tend his wounds.
Where pain is physical, we know what to do, and we
move quickly to staunch the flow of blood or cool the
fevered brow. We are not born with that knowledge. We
learn it early from watching others, from the welcome

coolness of a damp cloth on our own foreheads when we are very small.

But how does one apply a poultice to a bruised soul? We come into this world without that knowledge, too. And we do not come by it so early in life. As children we are shooed away from weeping adults; the soothing words they speak to one another fall unheard on our ears long after night has fallen and we have been tucked into our cots. When the greatest tragedy we can conceive is a broken toy or a lost kitten, we have no understanding of the greater sorrows life holds.

And so we grow up helpless. We say to the anguished, not "What can I do?", but "Let me know if there is anything I can do." Unwittingly we add to their burden, forcing them to tell us what they need. It is easier to rage at a silent God than to knock at a neighbor's door and ask to be allowed to weep! But ask we must; ask you must, my friends.

Job: Ah yes, I sat on the dump and begged God to come to me. I waited for my friends to seek me out, and only grew angry when they began to speak. I have much to ponder tonight, and I am weary. Can we close this day with prayer and seek rest?

Julian: It is fitting. Let us reflect on what we have known of compassion and then join our voices in praise of the God whose tender love sparks mercy in our own hearts.

For Reflection

- *What sense of God's compassion do you have? How have you gained it?*

- *Whose compassion has given you comfort? How did that person or persons learn compassion?*

- *What do you want someone to do for you? To whom can you express that need?*

- *Whose pain have you been able to ease? How did you bring comfort?*

- *Toward whom does your experience enable you to feel compassion?*

Closing Prayer

(Group response: "Praise the God of compassion.")

Praise the LORD!
Praise the LORD, O my soul!
I will praise the LORD as long as I live;
   I will sing praises to my God all my life long.

Do not put your trust in princes,
   in mortals, in whom there is no help.
When their breath departs, they return to the earth;
   on that very day their plans perish.

Happy are those whose help is the God of Jacob,
   whose hope is in the LORD their God,
who made heaven and earth,
   the sea, and all that is in them;
who keeps faith forever;
   who executes justice for the oppressed;
   who gives food to the hungry.

The LORD sets the prisoners free;
   the LORD opens the eyes of the blind.
The LORD lifts up those who are bowed down;

the LORD loves the righteous.
The LORD watches over the strangers;
 he upholds the orphan and the widow,
 but the way of the wicked he brings to ruin.

The LORD will reign forever,
 your God, O Zion, for all generations.
Praise the LORD!²³

Notes

¹ *Wind, Sand and Stars*, by Antoine de Saint Exupéry, translated from the French by Lewis Galantière, pp. 113, 118, 124-125, 127.

² Philippians 2:6-7.

³ See Matthew 25:31-46.

⁴ *Showings*, pp. 272-275, 277-278.

⁵ See Genesis 18:20-33.

⁶ Eucharistic Prayer IV.

⁷ *Showings*, pp. 224-225.

⁸ The Easter Proclamation, Easter Vigil liturgy, translation by International Commission for English in the Liturgy, Inc., Washington, D.C. (1970).

⁹ 1 Corinthians 1:22-25.

¹⁰ *Showings*, p. 149.

¹¹ *For Those I Loved*, by Martin Gray with Max Gallo, translated from French by Anthony White (Boston: Little, Brown and Company, 1971), p. 227.

¹² Gray, p. 244.

¹³ Job 2:6.

¹⁴ *Showings*, p. 165.

¹⁵ Ephesians 3:18-21.

¹⁶ See Matthew 25:31-40.

¹⁷ *Showings*, p. 340.

¹⁸ Romans 5:8.

¹⁹ *Showings*, pp. 262-263.

[20] *Showings*, p. 258.

[21] Job 30:24-25; 31:15.

[22] See Mark 10:51.

[23] Psalm 146.

Day Seven
Walking in Trust

Coming Together in the Spirit

The August sun shone hot on the Olympic stadium in Barcelona. Beneath its blaze young men fired by dreams of glory pushed strong bodies to the utmost in the 1992 400-meter semifinals. Suddenly one went down with a ruptured hamstring. A medical team raced onto the track, but Derek Redmond waved them away. Trouble with his Achilles tendons had kept the English lad out of the 1988 Olympics. Five operations and a lot of work later, he was not giving up. "There ain't no way I'm getting on that stretcher," he said. "I'm going to finish my race."

High in the stands, someone else started to run. A man shot past security guards, vaulted the wall onto the track and ran toward the fallen figure. As the crowd watched in amazement, Jim Redmond lifted his son and braced the young man's body with his own. Leaning hard against his dad, Derek hopped the last half of the track on one foot. The crowd screamed cheers as the pair crossed the finish line.

Derek finished last, of course. But, trusting the support of his dad's sturdy body and loving heart, he did finish. And he gained a prize struck of finer gold than an Olympic medal: the conviction of his father's love.

Defining Our Thematic Context

Complaining Job and serene Julian have something important in common: an abiding trust in God's willingness to hear human cries. In the course of this retreat, they have encouraged you to acknowledge the depth of your pain, to test the reasons conventional wisdom offers for human suffering, to rethink your concepts of God and God's ways, to plumb the reality of human brokenness, to look for support in the believing community and to let compassion grow from your scars.

Today, as they prepare to tell you good-bye, they speak of their own trust in God, and invite you to rest in it.

Opening Prayer

Job, voice of the suffering,
thank you for speaking for me.
Continue to inspire my prayer
with your determination.
Help me to persevere
until God hears me
and I hear the reply
God has been speaking all along.

Julian, kind visionary,
you have offered your showings
to all your brothers and sisters,
to me.
Grant me the wisdom to know
that experience ever needs deeper reflection,
to trust that God is near in joy and in woe.
Help me listen for the voice that tells me
all will indeed be well;

every manner of thing will be well.

Wise mentors,
continue to guide me
on my journey toward the God
who permits us to sorrow
but wills us everlasting joy.

RETREAT SESSION SEVEN

Julian: We have walked together these many days, and now we must prepare to part. My deepest wish for you is that you will be able to walk in trust. For it is God's will *that we have great trust in him, out of complete and true faith, for it is his will that we know he will appear, suddenly and blessedly, to all his lovers.... And he wants to be trusted, for he is very accessible, familiar and courteous, blessed may he be.*[1]

Job: To those whose days are bitter anguish, trust seems a leap into the darkness, a whisper flung against a furious wind. Do you not agree, friends?

Julian: Not I! The woe is the darkness; trust is a leap into the light that is God. Always and everywhere God's light surrounds us, even though our eye in its blindness perceives only the darkness of our sorrow. *For as the soul is clad in the cloth, and the flesh in the skin, and the bones in the flesh, and the heart in the trunk, we are clad and enclosed in the goodness of God. Yes, and more closely, for all these vanish and waste away; the goodness of God is always complete, and* *closer to us, beyond any comparison.*[2]

Job: Don't shake your finger at me, Mother Julian! I am no child; I am centuries older than you!

It was not God's absence that tormented my soul, but the fact that I could not escape divine attention. *"Let me alone,"* I prayed, *"that I may find a little comfort!"*[3] I prayed—God knows I prayed! I cried out day and night:

> Only grant two things to me,
>   then I will not hide myself from your face:
> withdraw your hand from me,
>   and do not let dread of you terrify me.
> Then call, and I will answer;
>   or let me speak, and you reply to me....
> Why do you hide your face
>   and count me as your enemy?[4]

Julian: Yet prayer itself bespeaks trust. People who truly believe that God will not hear them do not pray; only those who know his tender mercy and patience—even though that knowledge lies deep in their hearts, hidden from their understanding—dare to presume on the Lord's great courtesy and call God's name in prayer. You would not have prayed had you not trusted God even in your pain, Job. And surely, my friends, it was deep-down trust that brought you here to pray with Job and me.

But still our trust is often not complete, because we are not sure God hears us, as we think, because of our unworthiness and because we are feeling nothing at all; for often we are as barren and dry after our prayers as we were before....

Beseeching is a true and gracious, enduring will of the soul, united and joined to our Lord's will by the sweet, secret operation of the Holy Spirit. Our Lord himself is the first receiver of our prayer, as I see it, and he accepts it most thankfully, and greatly rejoicing he sends it up above, and puts it in a treasure house where it will never perish. It is there before God with all his holy saints, continually received, always furthering our needs.[5]

Job: I had thought of my prayer as something I needed, yet you say it is something the Lord treasures.

Julian: Job speaks two truths, my friends. One is that prayer is our need, especially when tribulations assail us. During my showings, I was not moved to beseech God for anything, but only to keep all the good things I saw in my mind. *But when we do not see God, then we need to pray, because we are failing, and for the strengthening of ourselves....*[6] For God does not change but is faithful and loving. We are so foolish and weak that we are blind to God; prayer opens our eyes.

The second truth is that our prayer is most precious in God's sight. God wishes us to pray because prayer unites us to God. *And so he teaches us to pray and to have firm trust...; for he beholds us in love, and wants to make us partners in his goodwill and work. And so he moves us to pray for what it pleases him to do....*[7] And what it pleases God to do is to comfort us and to make us know that we are enfolded most tenderly in his love.

Job: It was God's silence I railed against. I felt he had turned away from me for reasons I could not fathom. A terrible loneliness overcame me; I was a child abandoned by its mother, left to scream in rage and fear.

Julian: But when a tantrum overwhelms a little one, a wise mother does not sit down and reason with it. Rather, she sweeps it up in her arms and holds it close so it cannot hurt itself, rocking silently until the storm of

/

temper subsides. And God is a wise and loving mother. "Is there anyone among you," Jesus asks in my Bible, "who, if your child asks for bread, will give a stone? Or if the child asks for a fish, will give a snake? If you then, who are evil, know how to give good gifts to your children, how much more will your Father in heaven give good things to those who ask him!"[8]

Job: I know now that I misread God's silence. I heard in it a message of refusal, of disapproval, of uncaring condemnation.

Some mortal silences do carry such meaning: a hate-filled stare, a face turned away in anger. Yet mortals can also speak tenderly with silence. I remember my wife in our golden days silently snuggling her back against mine in the night, brushing my shoulder when she passed by me, winking over a nursing infant's head, quickly scanning my face at evenfall to judge how my day had gone. In a thousand wordless ways she said, "I am here. I love you," without uttering a word.

And for the seven days my friends sat quietly with me, I warmed myself in their nearness; I knew their compassion. Had they never spoken, they would have brought me only healing.

Julian: So it is with God, who stays nearer to us than any earthly friend or lover, who dwells in our souls in silent communion. *Greatly we ought to rejoice that God dwells in our soul; and more greatly ought we to rejoice that our soul dwells in God....*

We are enclosed in the Father,
and we are enclosed in the Son,
and we are enclosed in the Holy Spirit.
And the Father is enclosed in us,

the Son is enclosed in us,
and the Holy Spirit is enclosed in us,
all wisdom and all goodness,
one God, one Lord.[9]

"The Lord be with you," we tell one another at worship; "Good-bye—God be with you," we tell one another at parting. And our words are not an empty wish, but a bow to the truth: The Lord *is* with us; God *will* be with you. For so God has promised as long as he has had dealings with our kind.

And if he speaks but little, he scatters the evidence of his love as freely as an absentminded cook oversalting the soup (as my maidservant—bless her kind attention to my needs—sometimes did). God proclaims his love in the complex workings of nature, writing it up and down the pages of our lives.

Job: One need only look around to see it.

But ask the animals, and they will teach you;
    the birds of the air, and they will tell you;
ask the plants of the earth, and they will teach you;
    and the fish of the sea will declare to you.
Who among all these does not know
    that the hand of the LORD has done this?
In his hand is the life of every living thing
    and the breath of every human being.[10]

Job: Julian, was not the purr of the cat in your lap God's blessing sounding in your ears?

Julian: Indeed it was! He was as soft and warm beneath my hand as the love in which God enfolds me. Do you have pets whose company gives you ease, my friends? And do they not speak to you with rough tongue and eloquent tail of God's comforting presence? There are few pleasures as sweet as sitting in silence with an animal who responds with unspoken devotion.

The psalmist invites us to imitate our pets, to linger in God's silence and hear in it the pledge of his troth:

> "Be still, and know that I am God!
>   I am exalted among the nations,
>   I am exalted in the earth."
> The LORD of hosts is with us;
>   the God of Jacob is our refuge.[11]

And when we thus rest in God and in God's tender silence, we will know peace and love. *Peace and love are always in us, living and working, but we are not always in peace and love; but he wants us so to take heed that he is the foundation of our whole life in love, and furthermore he is our everlasting protector....*[12]

Job: My friends demanded peace of me. Prayer, they insisted, sounds sweet to God only when the words are mild. When I raged and argued and complained, they condemned me. They placed my name in the rolls of the wicked and urged repentance on me.

> Should your babble put others to silence,
>   and when you mock, shall no one shame you?[13]

But how could I pray with falsehood in my mouth? How could I say to the God who reads my heart that I was content with my bitter lot? To whom can I speak the truth of my soul if not to my Friend? I tell you still,

> as long as my breath is in me
>   and the spirit of God is in my nostrils,
> my lips will not speak falsehood,

and my tongue will not utter deceit.[14]

Julian: Nothing blocks our prayer more surely than our hesitation at speaking the truth. Once a woman drenched my window sill with her tears. The Black Death had robbed her of three children, and now the fearful buboes were swelling in her husband's groin. Neither her sorrow nor her fear brought her to my cell. She sought succor because she could not pray. Not even the dear words of the *Pater Noster* would come to her lips, no matter how she tried.

"Help me to pray, Mother Julian," she wept.

"What do you feel?" I asked her.

"Angry," she replied. "Angry that my children will never grow strong and tall. Angry that my husband, a fine, sturdy man, lies even now at death's door. Angry at this evil that sweeps through our land. And angry"—her voice fell to a whisper—"at God for permitting such woe."

But had she prayed her anger, lifted it to God for healing and consolation? Oh no, she dared not allow such feelings into her prayer!

I told her what the Lord Christ had showed to me: "*I am the ground of your beseeching.*"[15] By this I understand that our desire to pray is rooted in him; his Spirit groans in our hearts when we have no words.

And we can entrust our feelings freely to him, for he has known them all. He fell to the ground in fear and reluctance before his torment on Calvary, and so great was his anguish that his sweat fell to the ground as drops of blood. And he was angry, the Gospels say—not just when he drove the greedy traders out of the temple, but also when his enemies wanted to limit his compassion for a man with a withered hand because it was the sabbath day. Listen to the way my Bible tells it:

129

> Then he said to them, "Is it lawful to do good or to do harm on the sabbath, to save life or kill?" But they were silent. He looked around at them with anger; he was grieved at their hardness of heart....[16]

Anger can indeed become a grave sin when we choose it and nurture it and wish harm to another because of it. But first it is our nature, one of the sinews of the soul, as someone once called it. Anger is our response to pain, a strength we draw on when we are threatened. Even my cat, that most affectionate beast, snarls at me when I treat the injury he has met in a fight with another tom.

Job: I think we have come full circle. We began with giving names to the pains we feel, and now you ask us to entrust them to God in our prayer. Perhaps some of the reasons we explored on the second day will begin to have more meaning when we have worked our way through to them together with God.

Julian: I trust they will, for God so wishes it. It is God's will that we continue to seek most diligently so that even in our woe we may find joy in the love that enfolds us. *To any soul who sees the Creator of all things, all that is created seems very little.... [H]e who created it created everything for love, and by the same love it is preserved.... God is everything that is good, as I see, and the goodness which everything has is God.*[17]

Job: Yet suffering is the lot of mortals; we are broken by sin and sorrow. *Do not human beings have a hard service on earth...?*[18] But God tends our wounds if we allow it, if we know our helplessness and persistently turn to the Healer.

Julian: Yes, and he gives us one another in Holy Church so that we may lean on each other as we journey. In that good company we celebrate God's compassion; in that good company we discover that God has given each of us a gift that makes the divine image shine forth from us: the precious gift of compassion for others. And now God asks us to walk in trust.

Job: God has brought us together as companions on this journey. I hope we will meet again. If you seek my company, I am not hard to find. When you seat yourself in the dump, I will be there too, ready to weep with you and for you. I am the voice of suffering humanity. I will be your voice whenever you need words to hurl at God.

Julian: I too hope we will meet again. I have long since left my little cell in Norwich, though I stay close to it, for it was home to me for many years. I still like to visit it, to watch a cat prowl its grounds and remember the comfort the music of a purr brought to me.

I am still just beyond the curtain; it is only the curtain that has changed. Now I look out not at Norwich but at a planet no bigger than a hazelnut in God's hand. Call to me and I will hear you; I will listen. And I will tell you once more that all will be well. And you must trust my words, for now I truly know of what I speak.

Job: I said we have come full circle, for the path we have trod is truly circular. We come to its end and begin again, for pain will again wash over us; new sorrows will surely come our way.

Julian: Dear Job, you complain yet! Centuries older than I though you may be, you still sound to me a mewling child! Here, give Mother Julian your hand and let us walk on together.

Our path is not a circle but a spiral, ascending toward God. The Lord's promise lights our way: *Suddenly you will be taken out of all your pain, all your sickness, all your unrest and all your woe. And you will come up above, and you will have me for your reward, and you will be filled full of joy and bliss, and you will never again have any kind of pain, any kind of sickness, any kind of displeasure, no lack of will, but always joy and bliss without end.*[19]

And all shall be well, my friends. Ponder those words, which the Lord himself vouchsafed to me, before we join in prayer one more time.

For Reflection

- *What insights, what comfort have Julian and Job brought to you?*

- *How well have you come to know your mentors?*

- *With which one do you feel most comfortable? Why?*

- *Recall a time when silence spoke love to you. Relax in God's silence and join Julian and Job in prayer.*

Closing Prayer

(Group response: "My soul is calmed and quieted.")

O LORD, my heart is not lifted up,
　　my eyes are not raised too high;
I do not occupy myself with things
　　too great and too marvelous for me.

But I have calmed and quieted my soul,
   like a weaned child with its mother;
   my soul is like the weaned child that is with me.

O Israel, hope in the LORD
   from this time on and forevermore.[20]

Julian: Trusting in God's love, let us become part of
God's goodwill and work by praying, thanking, trusting
and rejoicing, for this is our loving Lord's wish for us.
The Lord gave me my showings because he wants us all
to know his will better, and he wants us to love him and
cling to him as a child clings to its mother's skirts.

For we are the treasure he looks on with sweet and
tender love while we are on earth. To us he pledges joy
and comfort in heavenly delight. Even now he would
draw our hearts from sorrow and darkness and have us
know consolation.

So I was taught that love is our Lord's meaning....
In this love we have our beginning,
   and all this shall we see in God without end.
   Thanks be to God.[21]

Job: O that my words were written down!
         O that they were inscribed in a book!
      O that with an iron pen and with lead
         they were engraved on a rock forever!
      For I know that my Redeemer lives,
         and that at the last he will stand upon the earth;
      and after my skin has been thus destroyed,
         then in my flesh I shall see God,
      whom I shall see on my side,
         and my eyes shall behold, and not another.
      My heart faints within me![22]

Julian: Pray now your own need, and for the needs of all your brothers and sisters, my friends....

And let us part with our gracious Lord's own words upon our lips: Our Father....

God wishes to be seen, and he wishes to be sought, and he wishes to be expected, and he wishes to be trusted.[23] For his will and pleasure is that all shall be well.

Glory be to the Father,
and to the Son,
and to the Holy Spirit,
world without end! Amen.

Notes

[1] *Showings*, p. 196.

[2] *Showings*, p. 186.

[3] Job 10:20b.

[4] Job 13:20-21, 24.

[5] *Showings*, pp. 248, 249.

[6] *Showings*, p. 159.

[7] *Showings*, p. 253.

[8] Matthew 7:9-11.

[9] *Showings*, p. 285.

[10] Job 12:7-10.

[11] Psalm 46:10-11.

[12] *Showings*, p. 245.

[13] Job 11:3.

[14] Job 27:3-4.

[15] *Showings*, p. 248.

[16] Mark 3:4-5a.

[17] *Showings*, p. 190.

[18] Job 7:1a.

[19] *Showings*, p. 306.
[20] Psalm 131.
[21] *Showings*, pp. 342-343.
[22] Job 19:23-27.
[23] *Showings*, p. 194.

Deepening Your Acquaintance

Deepening Your Acquaintance With Job:

The Book of Job. The translation used here is the *New Revised Standard Version*.

Job Speaks: The Book of Job in A Poet's Bible, interpreted from the Original Hebrew Book of Job by David Rosenberg. N.Y.: Harper & Row, Publishers, 1977.

J.B.: A Play in Verse, by Archibald MacLeish. Boston: Houghton Mifflin Company, 1956.

A Masque of Reason, by Robert Frost, in *The Collected Works of Robert Frost*, edited by Edward Connery Lathem. N.Y.: Holt, Rinehart and Winston, 1964.

Job and Jonah: Questioning the Hidden God, by Bruce Vawter, C.M. N.Y.: Paulist Press, 1983.

On Job: God-Talk and the Suffering of the Innocent, by Gustavo Gutiérrez. Translated from the Spanish by Matthew J. O'Connel. Maryknoll, N.Y.: Orbis Books, 1987.

Deepening Your Acquaintance With Julian:

Julian of Norwich: Showings, translated by Edmund Colledge, O.S.A., and James Walsh, O.S.A. Ramsey, N.J.: Paulist Press, 1978.

Enfolded in Love: Daily Readings With Julian of Norwich, translated by members of The Julian Shrine. N.Y.: The Seabury Press, 1981.

All Shall Be Well: Daily Readings From Julian of Norwich,

abridged and arranged by Sheila Upjohn. Harrisburg, Penn.: Morehouse Publishing, 1992.

Julian (video). Ramsey, N.J.: Paulist Press, 1985.